ONE WEEK LOAN

Better places to live

D1354851

Following the General Election in June 2001
the responsibilities of the former Department of
the Environment, Transport and the Regions
(DETR) in this area were transferred to the new
Department for Transport, Local Government
and the Regions (DTLR)

Department for Transport,
Local Government and the Regions
Eland House
Bressenden Place
London SW1E 5DU
Telephone 020 7944 3000
Web site: www.dtlr.gov.uk

Commission for Architecture &
The Built Environment
The Tower Building
11 York Road
London SE1 7NX
Telephone: 020 7960 2400
Web site: www.cabe.org.uk

Further copies of this publication are
available from:

T̶ Thomas Telford *Publishing*

The Customer Services Department
Thomas Telford Limited, Units I/K,
Paddock Wood Distribution Centre
Paddock Wood, Tonbridge
Kent TN12 6UU
Tel: 020 7665 2464
Fax: 020 7665 2245

Web site: www.thomastelford.com

ISBN 0 7277 3037 1

Printed in Great Britain by
Latimer Trend & Company Ltd, Plymouth
on material containing 75% post-consumer
waste and 25% ECF pulp.

September 2001

Contents

Foreword

1 The need for better housing design

Purpose of the guide	8
Who should read the guide	8
Making the change	10
Preparing the guide	12
Using the guide	13

2 Understanding the context

The bigger picture	16
Access to facilities	17
The site and immediate surroundings	19
A joined-up approach	21
Some key points	21

3 Creating a movement framework

Movement and place-making	24
Creating connections	25
Routes and functions	26
Walking and cycling	26
Public transport	27
Managing the traffic	29
Servicing the home	31
Some key points	31

4 Housing mix and neighbourhood

Creating mixed communities	34
Providing a range of housing opportunities	34
Integrating special needs and general housing	35
Supporting the community	36
Some key points	37

5 Housing layout and urban form

The importance of structure	40
Perimeter blocks	42
Other block structures	48
Street widths and enclosure	49
Setbacks	50
Solar orientation	51
Public, private and communal space	52
Designing for privacy	53
Creating a feeling of safety	54
Accommodating parking	55
Some key points	59

6 Space in and around the home

Thinking about space in and around the home	62
Density and space	62
Relating indoor and outdoor space	64
Flexibility, adaptability and change	66
Innovation	69
Some key points	69

7 Thoroughness in design

The importance of thoroughness	72
Building elements	73
Interface elements	75
Landscape	76
Consistency and continuing involvement	77
Some key points	79

Appendices – Case studies   80

Further reading	106
Acknowledgements	108

Foreword

Where people live has a major effect on their life. If where they live is well-planned, well-designed and well-managed, their quality of life is likely to be a great deal better than that of those who live elsewhere.

Yet too many housing estates are designed for nowhere in particular. They can be soulless and dispiriting. All too often they are not well-connected to local services and promote dependency on the car.

Our policy guidance for the planning of new housing sets out a blueprint for a new and better approach. It forges a new link between planning and design to produce better living environments. The prize is a better quality of life for all and the key is good design.

In *By Design*, the guide to better urban design we published last year, we demonstrated the fundamental principles that are common to good design and how these might be applied. We are now taking this a stage further by focusing on the attributes that underlie well-designed, successful residential environments. In drawing up this guide we have looked at a series of case studies, both of contemporary developments and places that have stood the test of time. What these places have in common is that they illustrate how better attention to good design can enhance the quality of life experienced in the environment of our homes. One of the clearest lessons is that places should be designed around people. People should always come first.

Better places to live challenges local authorities and developers to think more imaginatively about design and layout. It is not a manual to be applied by rote or a substitute for using skilled designers. It is about promoting greater flair in creating better places in which to live.

Lord Falconer of Thoroton QC
Minister for Housing,
Planning and Regeneration

Sir Stuart Lipton
Chairman
Commission for Architecture
& the Built Environment

01

The need for better housing design

- Purpose of the guide
- Who should read the guide
- Making the change
- Preparing the guide
- Using the guide

Purpose of the guide

Planning Policy Guidance Note 3: Housing (PPG3) sets out a radical new approach to planning for housing. It makes fundamental changes, both to the way we plan for new housing and the ambition we show for the places which we build. Priority is given to the development of urban brownfield sites before greenfield land. The old 'predict and provide' approach to housing need has been abandoned and a new policy of Plan, Monitor and Manage has been introduced. Underlining all this is the central concern that planning for housing should be about people, places and our environment.

PPG3 requires new development of the highest quality. It looks for the best use to be made of the land we have available and for new development to be built in a sustainable way, sensitive to the needs of people and the impact it has on the environment. It reflects the principle that where we live affects how we live, and the emphasis of both the urban and rural white papers that better planning and design offers the prospect of a higher quality of life and opportunity for all. In short, it demands the step-change in quality required to break the mould of mediocrity that has characterised so much new housing development.

The purpose of this guide is to help deliver that change. It does not set out new policy, rather it is a companion to PPG3 and should be read alongside it. It is a guide to better practice, not a pattern book. The guide aims to prompt greater attention to the principles of good design, not constrain thought. It complements *By Design*[1] and *Places, Streets and Movement*[2] by drawing together the principles of good urban design as they relate to the residential environment. Its focus is the urban design principles and approaches which underpin successful housing, not architectural treatment. Only by giving attention to these principles can the quality of housing layout and design be raised.

There is much to learn from the urban design principles which underpin places which have worked over time and which remain popular today. Jesmond, Newcastle

Who should read the guide

The guide is aimed at all those involved in the planning, design and development of new housing but, in particular, at local planning and highway authorities, housebuilders and their professional advisors. It is relevant to the whole spectrum of housing, but a major focus is housing within the density range of 30 to 50 dwellings per hectare. The greatest challenge to current practice lies in improving the quality of the 'anywhere, everywhere' residential environments that, typically, have been built at around 20 to 25 dwellings per hectare.

Modern apartments combining good design with innovation in construction. Murray Grove, Hackney

PPG3 focuses development onto previously-developed land in urban areas, but the guide will be equally relevant for those working to improve the quality of new housing elsewhere, including on the urban fringe. Too often development on the edge of our towns has not only exhibited some of the poorest standards of layout and design, but also has failed to support sustainable lifestyles.

The guide highlights many examples of best practice in a wide range of areas. The lessons to be drawn from them are not unique to the locations where they are found. They have an application to *all* new housing development.

This guide can help produce better design. But designing attractive, sustainable and inclusive places which can be enjoyed by all who use them, including elderly and disabled people, depends on the skills of designers. This requires a culture of investing in design. And it means designing for a particular place and the needs of future residents.

The hope is that the better practice highlighted will act as a spur for further innovation among those at the cutting edge of housing design and construction.

Urban apartments grouped around a shared green space. Here homes, landscape, routes for movement and parking are blended seamlessly together to create an attractive and distinctive place to live. Barons Court, Hammersmith and Fulham

The principles of urban design

The fundamental principles of urban design are described more fully in *By Design*. They involve expressing the main objectives of urban design through the various aspects of the built form.

The objectives of urban design can be summarised as follows:

Character
- A place with its own identity

Continuity and Enclosure
- A place where public and private spaces are clearly distinguished

Quality of the Public Realm
- A place with attractive and successful outdoor areas

Ease of Movement
- A place that is easy to get to and move through

Legibility
- A place that has a clear image and is easy to understand

Adaptability
- A place that can change easily

Diversity
- A place with variety and choice

The aspects of the built form are described as follows:

- Layout: Urban Structure – the framework of routes and spaces that connect locally and more widely, and the way developments, routes and open spaces relate to one another
- Layout: Urban Grain – the pattern of the arrangement of street blocks, plots and their buildings in a settlement
- Landscape – the character and appearance of land, including its shape, form, ecology, natural features, colours and elements, and the way these components combine
- Density and Mix – the amount of development on a given piece of land and the range of uses. Density influences the intensity of development, and, in combination with the mix of uses, can affect a place's vitality and viability.
- Scale: Height – scale is the size of a building in relation to its surroundings, or the size of parts of a building or its details, particularly in relation to the size of a person. Height determines the impact of development on views, vistas and skylines
- Scale: Massing – the combined effect of the arrangement, volume and shape of a building or group of buildings in relation to other buildings and spaces
- Appearance: Details – the craftsmanship, building techniques, decoration, styles and lighting of a building or structure
- Appearance: Materials – the texture, colour, pattern and durability of materials, and how they are used

The need for better housing design

Making the change

PPG3 lays down a clear challenge both to housebuilders and to local authorities to take design seriously. Good design is not an extra that can be ignored, it is central to creating more attractive living environments and central to delivering sustainable developments through:

- making more efficient use of land;
- promoting better accessibility to local facilities and public transport;
- supporting crime prevention and community safety;
- creating more socially inclusive communities;
- promoting energy efficiency.

Many new housing developments fall short of what can be expected from the new approach set out in PPG3. There has been a growing gap between the exemplars of best practice and the standards achieved in the majority of cases.

Most recent housing developments have wasted land. PPG3 reported that more than half of new housing was developed at densities of less than 20 dwellings per hectare. As a consequence, many places fail to sustain local facilities and public transport.

All too frequently, inadequate thought has been given to safe, direct and convenient walking and cycling routes and insufficient attention has been paid to the relationship of spaces within and around the home. Too many housing developments have turned their backs on the wider community and have focused instead on narrowly defined markets and housing types. Communities are the poorer for it.

The responsibility for the unsustainable places that have resulted from poor design does not rest solely at the housebuilder's door. Underlying many of these shortcomings is a combination of local authority planning and highway design standards. These have helped give impetus to the palette of standard house types and layout forms which have been developed to meet these requirements. The result has been residential environments that meet these standards but lack any real quality or distinctive sense of place.

Typical suburban housing 1990's style with houses arranged around a road network designed for the car. Layouts such as this use land inefficiently and make viable public transport almost impossible

Cities Revealed® aerial photography copyright Get Mapping.com™ 1999

The main route into a new neighbourhood. Everyone passes along it, yet the houses turn their backs onto it. The result is a soulless place where pedestrians feel insecure and where drivers are 'encouraged' to drive fast

Housing which met planning and highway design standards, but which wastes space and fails to create any sense of place or identity

Standard house types developed without proper regard for their context and setting. This scheme misses the opportunity to optimise housing capacity and undermines the character of the existing street

PPG3 provides the opportunity of a fresh start through:

- requiring local authorities to review critically the standards they apply to new development, particularly in relation to road layouts and car parking provision;
- encouraging more efficient use of land (housing development in the range of 30 to 50 dwellings to the hectare net) and higher densities where there is good accessibility to local facilities and public transport;
- requiring a better, and more appropriate mix of dwelling size, type and affordability in new development;
- looking to applicants for planning permission to demonstrate how they have taken into account the need for good urban design and making it clear that local planning authorities should reject poor design.

Delivering a fundamental change in the quality and layout of new residential environments requires investment in design and the appropriate design skills being brought to bear at the right time. Above all, it requires a better understanding of the design principles which contribute to the creation of successful residential environments. This is the purpose of this guide.

Efficient housing forms, such as the terrace, can be interpreted in very different ways and can meet a range of different housing requirements. What is common to both examples is the creation of a coherent urban form and a commitment to quality design. Lickey Hills, Birmingham (top) Millennium Village, Greenwich (below)

The need for better housing design

Preparing the guide

Unlike previous design guides which have relied heavily on a singular view of housing design, this guide takes a more reflective approach. This is based on the view that:

- the shortcomings in current practice are first and foremost to do with basic issues of layout rather than detailed issues of internal configuration, construction materials or architectural idiom;
- we can learn from the best of contemporary practice, but we can also learn a great deal from those residential environments which have stood the test of time, met the housing needs and expectations of many generations and which remain popular today;
- the residential environment must be seen in the round; approaches which have given too much emphasis to one issue (notably to accommodating traffic) have often failed because they departed from other tried and tested principles of urban design.

This guide is based on a detailed examination of both historic and contemporary practice, drawing from a study of residential environments from across the country. While a number of the developments included in the guide have won Housing Design Awards[3] for the quality of their design, the guide deliberately draws from a wide range of different housing forms and contexts rather than looking solely at the very best of contemporary British housing design. The residential environments were selected to provide clear examples of practical approaches to implementing the basic principles of good urban design in a variety of different contexts, and to highlight both strong and weak points in their design. Indeed, an important objective in their selection was to include representation of ordinary, everyday housing as a counterfoil to some of the better known examples. The architecture illustrated in the guide will not, therefore, be to everyone's taste.

The focus has been the attributes of successful housing environments. These are the transferable lessons that can contribute to the creation of better residential environments in a wide variety of different contexts.

The attributes of successful housing

A literature review and analysis of historic and contemporary practice identified a number of attributes of successful housing. These were tested by a sounding board drawing on expertise from a wide range of disciplines working in a variety of backgrounds - including architects, highway engineers, landscape architects, planners, house builders and police officers concerned with crime prevention. These attributes provided a basis for the analysis of selected residential environments and are reflected in the structure and content of the guide. The attributes are set out below, together with a signposting to the relevant Chapters of the guide.

		Chapters
Movement	A movement framework which is safe, direct and attractive to all users	2, 3 & 5
Mix	A rich mix of housing opportunities	4
Community	A sense of neighbourhood and community ownership	2 & 4
Structure	A coherent structure of buildings, spaces, landscape and routes for movement	3 & 5
Layout	Street layout and design which is appropriate to use and context	3 & 5
Place	Attractive and clearly defined public and private spaces	5, 6 & 7
Amenity	Pleasant gardens and private amenity space	6 & 7
Parking	Convenient but unobtrusive car parking	5 & 7
Safety	A safe and secure environment	All
Space	Well planned homes which provide space and functionality	6
Adaptability	Housing which is robust and adaptable to changing requirements	6
Maintenance	An environment which can be well maintained over the long-term	6 & 7
Sustainability	Housing designed to minimise resource consumption	All
Detail	Well considered detailing of buildings and spaces	7

Using the guide

The places which feature in this guide provide many important, and often straightforward, lessons that are relevant and applicable to new housing development across the country. But the examples used are not presented as either the Government's or CABE's preferred view of architectural treatment, construction practices or social mix. Nor should the places drawn upon in the guide be treated as model templates that can or should be copied in a simplistic manner. That would defeat the aim of this guide.

The guide has been written to prompt a holistic view of the design of residential environments. It is ordered to reflect the necessary layering of analysis from understanding the context for development through to concerns of detailed design. For ease of use, it brings together within individual chapters particular attributes of successful housing. Other attributes of fundamental importance - safety and security, robustness and adaptability, management and environmental performance - are over-arching concerns which permeate each level of analysis.

The guide is divided into six further chapters as follows:

- Understanding the context
  (Chapter 2)
- Creating a movement framework
  (Chapter 3)
- Housing mix and neighbourhood
  (Chapter 4)
- Housing layout and urban form
  (Chapter 5)
- Space in and around the home
  (Chapter 6)
- Thoroughness in design
  (Chapter 7)

Each chapter concludes with a short checklist setting out the key questions to be addressed if successful residential environments are to be secured. The guide is supported by an Appendix which provides detailed information and comparative data on the case study areas.

End notes:

1 *By Design. Urban design in the planning system: towards better practice*

2 *Places, Streets and Movement: A companion guide to Design Bulletin 32 Residential roads and footpaths*

3 The Housing Design Awards are sponsored by the Department for Transport, Local Government and the Regions, the National House–Building Council, the Royal Institute of British Architects and the Royal Town Planning Institute. They are presented annually for projects or completed schemes of four or more dwellings which reflect the highest standards in housing design.

02
Understanding the context

- The bigger picture
- Access to facilities
- The site and immediate surroundings
- A joined-up approach
- Some key points

'New housing development of whatever scale should not be viewed in isolation. Considerations of design and layout must be informed by the wider context, having regard not just to any immediate neighbouring buildings but the townscape and landscape of the wider locality.'

PPG 3: Housing paragraph 56

The bigger picture

The successful integration of new housing with its surrounding context is a key design objective, irrespective of whether a site lies on the urban fringe or at the heart of a town centre. A crucial first step in achieving this is to develop a thorough understanding of the context within which the new housing will sit and then of the nature of the site itself and its immediate surroundings. This initial analysis will inform a whole range of subsequent design decisions including, for example:

- scale and massing of development;
- framework for movement;
- mix of dwelling types and sizes;
- landform, landscape and ecology of the site;
- orientation of dwellings;
- mix of uses and provision of community facilities;
- amount and arrangement of car parking.

While contextual analysis has traditionally focused on issues such as landscape, townscape and the use of appropriate materials, the objectives of sustainable development and urban renaissance now require a broader approach. In particular, greater emphasis now needs to be given to the linkages between new housing and:

- local facilities and community infrastructure;
- the public transport network;
- established walking and cycling routes.

Making these linkages is fundamental to achieving more sustainable patterns of movement and to reducing people's reliance on the car. Understanding a site's relationship to local facilities and to the public transport network is therefore not only an important element of contextual appreciation, it is also central to the consideration of the extent to which a site may be appropriate for higher density development in the context of the guidance given in PPGs 3 and 13.

This chapter illustrates the form that contextual analysis can take in a variety of different places. It gives particular emphasis to accessibility on foot to local facilities and the public transport network, but also highlights other contextual considerations[1].

Site

New housing sensitively integrated into the established urban grain. Webster's Yard, Kendal

Here the new housing layout is informed by surrounding historic routes and the desire to create good communal spaces. Friars Quay, Norwich

Access to facilities

Most urban sites have very rich settings comprising existing communities, historic movement patterns, a mix of uses and activities and many generations of investment in community infrastructure, technical services and facilities.

Having established a site's broad setting in terms of its relationship to a city, town or village centre, a good starting point is to examine the area within 10 minutes' (about 800m) walking distance of the site. This can help to identify the range of facilities which residents may access comfortably on foot, as well as opportunities to reach more distant facilities by public transport.

The diagram of the Stanstead Road area below illustrates how such analysis can be applied to one of the case study areas in a mature inner suburb. Quality of access should be assessed in terms of distance and routes to local services, including shops, schools, general practitioners' surgeries and so on.

In practice, this would be supported by analysis of the frequency of bus and train services and an assessment of the quality of pedestrian routes to all local destinations in terms of their safety, quality, gradients and crossing points. The study *Sustainable Residential Quality: exploring the housing potential of large sites*[2] includes case study analysis illustrating aspects of such appraisal.

Analysis of the provision of local facilities and services in the area around a site is also an important first step in considering the opportunities to provide new community facilities as part of the development. These issues are considered further in Chapter 4.

Contextual analysis of this type is simple and straightforward, but it can alter significantly perceptions of the development potential of a site, for example by demonstrating that it is much better served by facilities and public transport than may have been apparent from a cursory inspection.

Simple but informative analysis of a site's relationship to local facilities and the public transport network. This analysis of a site in a mature inner suburb used 1:10,000 scale mapping and was conducted as a desk exercise with a follow-up site visit. The analysis points to a site which is better served by local facilities and public transport than may have been apparent from a more instinctive analysis. Stanstead Road, Lewisham

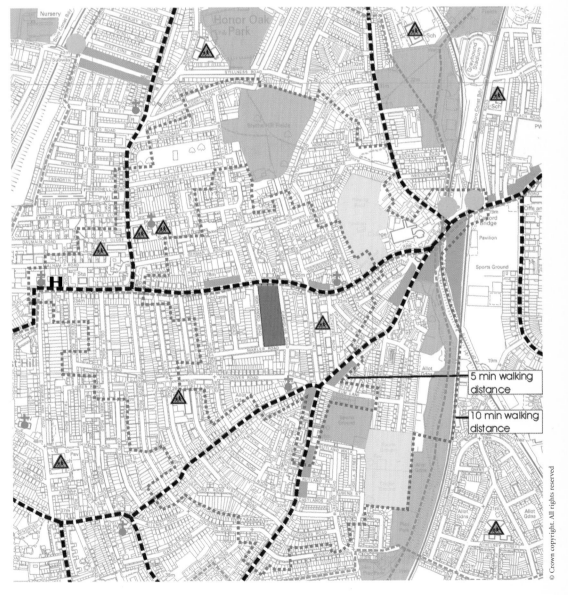

| | 5 min walking distance |
| | 10 min walking distance |

Site	
Local shops	
Public open space	
Open space	
Bus route	∎∎▪
Place of worship	✝
Railway station	●
School	▲
Health Facility	H
Cycle route	----

Housing development on the edge of an urban area can present particular challenges. The issue is how to knit new development into the existing urban fabric, which may not have been planned with future expansion in mind. Even where it has, developers and local authorities may come under pressure from local residents to propose access arrangements which are neither sustainable nor suited to the new development. These problems can be difficult, but a positive approach is needed if long-term issues of sustainable movement are not to be sacrificed for short-term convenience.

Issues of a more strategic nature arise where housing is being planned as part of a major urban extension. Here the issues are not only to do with direct connections, but also with ensuring that the new development is complementary in scale and function to the existing settlement. In particular, planned urban extensions can provide opportunities to enhance the quality and frequency of bus services to and from the town centre. Such improvements will benefit not just new residents, but all those living and working along the route[3].

The forthcoming publication *Planning and Sustainable Access* (DTLR 2001) provides more detailed consideration of both the strategic and detailed issues to be addressed in planning for access by a range of travel modes.

New housing on the urban edge making the connections (shown by arrows) with existing movement patterns. Poundbury, Dorchester

Poundbury has been designed as a mixed community of 5,000 people on the outskirts of Dorchester. The intention is to complement rather than compete with the existing town centre, where the major facilities (the market, hospital and principal shops) are located. The new development has a variety of facilities, including workplaces and shops for everyday items, but for many of their needs residents travel the short distance to the traditional centre.

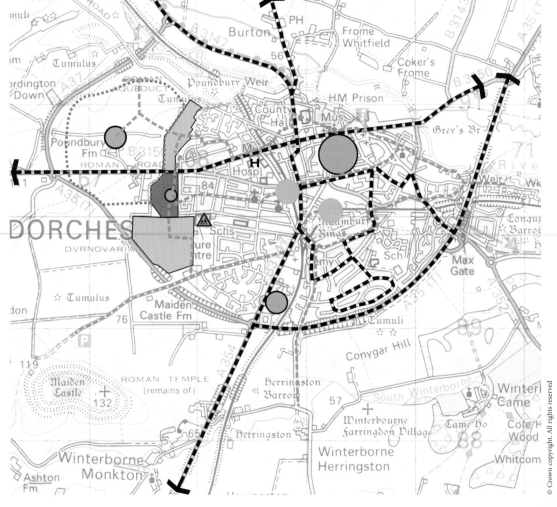

Site	▪
Proposed expansion	⬚
Local shops	▨
Open space	▨
Bus route	- - -
Cycle route	·····
Place of worship	⚲
Railway station	●
School	▲
Health Facility	H

The site and immediate surroundings

Understanding the opportunities and constraints presented by the site and its more immediate surroundings is a well established aspect of development appraisal.

The analysis of a site's immediate surroundings will include an assessment of:

- landform and ecology;
- established building heights;
- landmark buildings or important landscape features;
- pedestrian desire lines around and through the site;
- views into and through the site;
- orientation of the fronts and backs of buildings adjoining the site;
- hostile edges, 'bad-neighbour' uses and areas of positive aspect;
- availability and capacity of utilities and other services.

In addition, Crime Pattern Analysis can help ensure that the layout and design of new housing are informed by analysis of criminal activity in an area and contribute to crime reduction objectives[4].

The analysis of the site itself will include considerations such as:

- landscape structure and the presence of mature trees;
- important views out from the site;
- physical constraints such as ground contamination, overhead power lines or steep slopes etc;
- potential open space areas.

Fuller consideration is given to these and other aspects of contextual analysis in *By Design*[5].

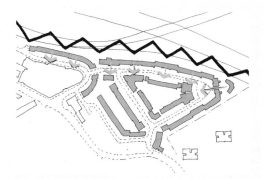

∨∨ Railway line　　**→** Front aspect

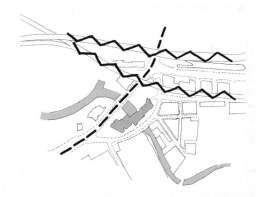

Here orientating the fronts of dwellings away from a dominating railway line is an important structuring element in the design. Isledon Village, Islington

∨∨ Railway bridge
- - - - Major traffic route

A robust design response to an environment dominated by elevated railway lines, roads and substantial buildings. Deansgate Quay, Manchester

Integrating new housing with a mature urban landscape

The canopies of trees have an impressive relationship to the roof line of houses

Tree trunks are seen as part of the building elevation

New planting has been introduced to soften building elements

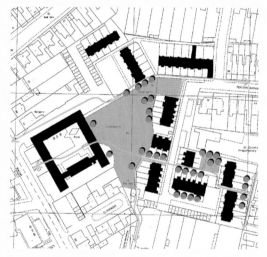

- ■ **Dwellings**
- ▨ **Open space**
- — **Pedestrian routes**
- ● **Mature trees**

Highsett demonstrates the quality of environment which can be created when the relationship between mature landscaping and new housing is considered in detail. The site was previously a backland area within a large urban block containing mature deciduous trees, open space and an orchard.

The layout and articulation of buildings have been heavily influenced by the location of established trees. For example:
- ■ buildings are arranged parallel to lines of trees;
- ■ special trees are organised to become a set-piece within small informal greenspaces;
- ■ pedestrian routes are organised to follow lines of established trees.

In particular, new planting has helped to soften edges of some parts of the architecture, such as where creepers have been introduced along end gables as well as helping to define the front boundaries of houses.

It is interesting to note that while, in general, guidance on the siting and design of open spaces (including that given in Chapters 4 and 5) emphasises the importance of buildings overlooking open space to provide good surveillance, Highsett shows that it is possible to depart from such principles.

However, it is important to appreciate that the open spaces at Highsett work within the context of a small and intimate development which is enclosed within a larger block. Hence the spaces are not subject to intensive use or general public access. As always, much depends on the skills of designers and in tailoring the design to the particular characteristics of the site and its surroundings.

The very close proximity at Highsett between some buildings and trees also requires very careful attention. In such cases great care is needed throughout the development process to ensure that trees survive the building phase and have enough space to spread their routes and branches over time[6].

Within the context of established trees, new planting has been introduced to renew the stock of larger species and to provide a contrasting scale of landscape.

Endnotes:

1 Indicator 1 (Location) of The Housing Quality Indicators can provide a helpful tool for conducting this part of the contextual analysis.

2 See pages 65 et seq.

3 Sustainable Urban Extensions: Planned through Design (September 2000), a joint publication by the Prince's Foundation, English Partnerships, DETR and the Council for the Protection of Rural England, provides further advice on designing urban extensions. See also the example illustrated on page 28.

4 Crime Pattern Analysis is carried out by the Police and is available through liaison with the Architectural Liaison Officer/Crime Prevention Design Advisor.

5 See pages 36-40. The Urban Design Compendium also has useful material and readers may also wish to refer to the Urban Design Alliance's Placecheck as an approach to contextual analysis.

6 Further guidance can be found in BS 5837: Trees in Relation to Construction.

A joined-up approach

Most experienced designers will undertake contextual analysis instinctively, building it into the design development process in an intuitive way. However, there can be real benefits in recording this analysis so that the emerging design approach can be related back to the initial appreciation. This can enable the wide range of people with an interest in the development to understand the design approach and to contribute to its development and refinement.

The purpose of contextual analysis is to make a positive contribution to the process of design development. For this to be effective it is important that the different elements of analysis are conducted in an integrated and informative way, rather than commissioned as discrete packages at different stages in the development process.

Design reviews, bringing together expertise from a range of different disciplines (as well as representation from local community groups, local authority access officers and other stakeholders), can play an important part in developing an holistic approach to the design process and ensuring that new housing is properly integrated with its surroundings. In this way contextual analysis can inform design development at all levels, from the orientation of routes for movement (see Chapter 3) to issues of detailed architectural treatment (see Chapter 7).

Some key points

In terms of the particular issues examined in this chapter, the following key points should be considered:

Access to facilities and public transport

- Has an adequate analysis been carried out of the site's relationships to public transport and local facilities?
- How has this analysis informed the design of the development? For example, in terms of density, car parking provision and pedestrian routes and entrances?
- Does the development accommodate important pedestrian desire lines through the site?
- How does the provision of facilities relate to existing provision in the surrounding area?

Townscape and landscape

- How does the development respond to its context in terms of building heights, setbacks, use of materials and the established urban grain?
- Has the potential of landform and local ecology been reflected in the layout?
- Does it maintain important views of prominent buildings or landscape features?

03
Creating a movement framework

- Movement and place-making
- Creating connections
- Routes and functions
- Walking and cycling
- Public transport
- Managing the traffic
- Servicing the home
- Some key points

Movement and place-making

The success or failure of a new development depends significantly on how well connected it is to existing areas, especially in terms of access to local services. That is why, in the contextual analysis of a proposed site, the question of how it will link to established routes and facilities is so important. Communities of every shape and size have always relied on movement as their lifeblood, both within their area and in linking them to the wider world.

It is all too easy, however, for movement to seem an end in itself, shaping a development to the exclusion of other factors. This is particularly detrimental when one form of movement is given priority above others, as happens when a road layout designed largely to the requirements of vehicular traffic is allowed to dictate the whole character of a development. Roads, streets and other routes have a multitude of functions in addition to carrying traffic. As described in *Places, Streets and Movement*, places which have stood the test of time are those where traffic and other activities have been successfully integrated and where the buildings and spaces, and needs of people, not just of their vehicles, shape the area. Successful environments are those designed at the human scale with the needs of pedestrians in mind.

The rigidity and standardisation of most recent housing layouts are partly the result of the dominance of motor vehicles. Layouts have been based on the geometry of vehicle movement, with the natural result that residents find it easier to use their car than any other form of travel. In these circumstances the car is immensely convenient. But there are many journeys made by car which, with better planning, could be made by walking, cycling or public transport. The layout of housing development can have a significant influence on that choice.

Whether it be infill or edge-of-town development, the quality of new housing depends on a movement framework based on the following considerations:
- the integration of new development into existing routes;
- provision for the maximum choice in how people make their journeys;
- the control of vehicle movement and speed;
- the design of routes which reinforce the character of the place;
- the location of shops and services near to new housing.

Roads, streets and other routes have a multitude of functions in addition to carrying traffic. Here houses, gardens, landscape and parking are integrated with movement routes for cars and pedestrians

A road designed primarily to carry traffic. Not only is it a soulless place, but its value to pedestrians as a safe walking route is also undermined by a lack of surveillance from nearby houses

The way each form of movement is provided for, namely the location of bus stops, walking distance to facilities, and the design of vehicle routes, is fundamental to the shaping of developments. This Chapter looks at how these priorities have been met with reference to the case study areas. The issues of traffic and movement are often thought to be insoluble, but evidence from schemes across the country shows just how much is possible even in the most challenging locations. The emphasis here is on general layout principles rather than on technical detail, which is already considered in *Places, Streets and Movement*.

The principles illustrated here are compatible with these technical requirements. Whatever the site or size of development, provision for the mobility of disabled and visually impaired people should always be made where new build is concerned, especially in the design of footways, crossings, parking (see Chapter 5) and access to front doors.

Creating connections

Routes should lead where people want to go. Providing for the optimum variety of journeys means creating open-ended, well-connected layouts. Introverted, dead-end layouts limit people's choice of how to travel, especially if they want to walk, cycle or use the bus. They also limit the adaptation or extension of the development. By contrast, a well-connected layout has many advantages:

- frequent points of access into and through the development;
- more convenient, direct routes for pedestrians and cyclists;
- better opportunities for the provision of bus services through the site;
- clear views and easy orientation;
- traffic dispersal;
- scope in the long-term for adaptation and change.

There is no standard formula for designing such layouts: much will depend on the local context (including local security issues) and how the development relates to existing areas.

The case studies demonstrate that these benefits can be achieved on almost every kind of site. For instance, Canning Street, Liverpool represents a traditional grid layout, providing a hierarchy of clear connections which work as well today as when the area was developed in the early nineteenth century. At Rolls Crescent, Manchester, a major regeneration project has been used to re-establish routes severed by insensitive 1960s development, thus knitting the area back into the city. Poundbury exemplifies how an edge-of-town community can be laid out to maximise access and allow for future expansion.

In essence, these and other examples illustrate two kinds of movement framework:

- *infill developments*: the maintenance or extension of existing routes to create a permeable layout. A well-planned development can help link together the areas that surround it;
- *edge-of-town developments*: the creation of a layout which provides a series of connections to the existing area and can easily be extended.

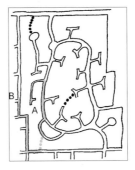

In this layout the journey from A to B is a long convoluted one. It does not allow for easy pedestrian journeys to neighbouring facilities, making a car trip more likely to get from A to B

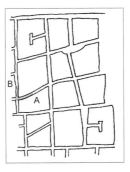

In this layout the journey from A to B is short, legible and direct. It encourages pedestrian journeys to local facilities as the preferred option

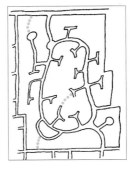

Pedestrian routes introduced to overcome poor connections often result in routes which are not overlooked and are unattractive to pedestrians

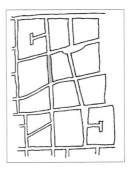

Pedestrian-only routes should be designed as an integral part of the street network, as here

Routes and functions

The types of road and street which form a movement framework are crucial in determining the character of a development. Conventionally, in recent years, their size and layout have been based on estimates of vehicle capacity, rather than on their overall, multi-functional role. As well as disadvantaging other street users, especially pedestrians and cyclists, this has resulted in the segregation of uses. Main routes have been diverted around development and major uses (including retail facilities) located along those routes. This fragmentation of the role of traditional streets detracts from the viability of small-scale uses, such as shops and services, which rely on a local, predominantly walk-in, catchment.

A traditional street hierarchy as, for instance, in the Canning Street area of Liverpool, is a reminder that to have main routes passing through rather than around the edge of an area helps sustain a variety of uses and connections. It enhances the viability of bus provision and the mutual support between public transport and other facilities. Only when traffic levels on the principal route threaten to sever an area is it necessary to consider the need for alternative routes.

▓▓▓   **Main routes**

B   **Bus stops**

**Main routes pass through the area, not around it.
Canning Street, Liverpool**

Walking and cycling

If people are to be persuaded to leave their cars at home, the routes for walking and cycling demand particular attention. Because they are simple, low-key modes of travel requiring no complex infrastructure, they are all too easily neglected. In fact, the design of new housing can benefit greatly from specialist design skills in respect of both walking and cycling.

Pedestrians and cyclists need routes which are positive, safe, direct, accessible and free from barriers. Generally streets which are designed for low traffic speeds are safe for walking and cycling (ideally 20mph or less), especially when the detailed layout design (of junctions, crossings and surfacing) has their needs in mind. People feel safer on streets where there is activity, where they can be seen by drivers, residents and other users.

New housing fronting the street ensures that routes are clearly overlooked. Calne, Wiltshire

**Routes are shared with footways clearly marked.
Friars Quay, Norwich**

Segregated pedestrian or cycle routes are not necessarily the answer, except when they can provide a more direct route from one place to another than the road. Only a few of the case studies incorporate segregated routes, and then only for very short distances. The success of most examples is based on their low speed environment, combined with the clarity of their layouts. Both Poundbury, Dorchester and Thorley Lane, Bishops Stortford illustrate how pedestrians and vehicles can coexist in shared-surface streets, generally designed to serve ten houses or fewer[1].

Shared-surface access serving a small group of dwellings. Thorley Lane, Bishops Stortford

A bonus to cycling is a street layout which restricts traffic movement but allows a through route for cyclists and pedestrians, a link which is a continuation of the street rather than a segregated route. Within such links there should be a clear demarcation between the cycle and pedestrian paths.

Cycles and cars can share the same movement space on streets with low traffic speeds. Greenland Passage, Southwark

Public transport

The idea of new housing linked to a railway station or a tram route, as so often happened in the nineteenth century, is still a real possibility. But for most developments it is the bus that matters. A crucial aspect of the connection between new and old development is the diversion or extension of an existing bus route, or the introduction of a new one.

Putting to one side issues of subsidy, a certain critical mass of development is needed to justify a regular bus service at frequent intervals, sufficient to provide a real alternative to the car. This will vary with context and route characteristics, but assuming stops at every 200-300 metres, ideally this means densities above 40 dwellings per hectare, preferably with increased densities around the stops[2].

Higher density housing along a public transport route supports a frequent bus service. Essex Road, Islington

The planning of the routes and location of stops are also crucial. The case studies and other evidence highlight that bus use depends on:
- routes which follow principal roads or streets through the heart of the area;
- stops located where activity is concentrated, near shops or a road junction;
- clear walking routes to the stops, including road crossings.

None of the case studies included a bus priority route, but that is not to say that one should not be considered, especially for large-scale schemes.

Integrating new housing on urban edge with improvements in public transport services

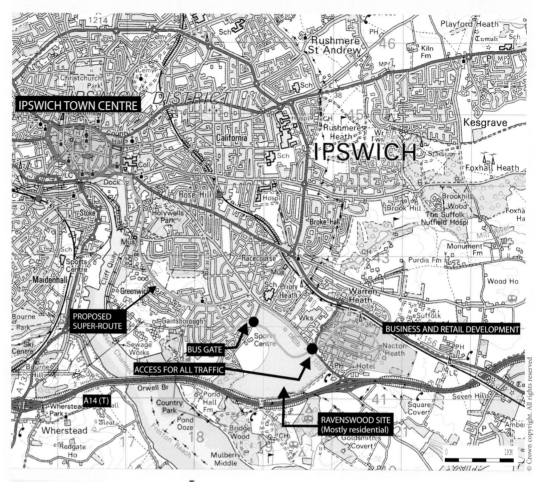

Labels on map:
- IPSWICH TOWN CENTRE
- IPSWICH
- PROPOSED SUPER-ROUTE
- BUS GATE
- ACCESS FOR ALL TRAFFIC
- BUSINESS AND RETAIL DEVELOPMENT
- RAVENSWOOD SITE (Mostly residential)

A new urban extension in Ipswich is being planned together with enhanced bus services to the town centre. The high quality, high profile Superoute service will be introduced over four years as the development is completed to provide an ultimate frequency of four buses an hour. The route has journey-generating uses at each end and an established residential area in between. This generates a two-way peak-flow and off-peak usage. The accessibility provided by the Superoute is contributing to the developer's marketing of the development.

Creating a movement framework

Managing the traffic

The varied uses of a typical street or road may help provide interest, but may also be a source of potential conflict, especially between vehicles and other users. The resolution of these problems lies in using a combination of three approaches:

- the design of the overall block structure and layout, including the length of streets and the spacing of junctions. This aspect is discussed further in Chapter 5;
- the management of traffic flows through the street network;
- the control of traffic speed.

Most housing areas are designed to concentrate the main traffic flows onto main roads, but traffic can have an adverse effect on subsidiary streets and roads unless through routes are restricted. The issue is how to restrict traffic without disadvantaging the free movement of pedestrians and cyclists.

Canning Street, Liverpool illustrates how selective street closures in a historic layout achieves a balance between vehicles and other users passing through the area. The same technique is equally valid in new development. The barrier to vehicles does not constitute a dead end, but is a natural part of the street overlooked by buildings. If necessary, a barrier can be in the form of removable or retractable bollards, to allow emergency vehicles and disabled badge holders to get through, or rumble strips which can be crossed by a fire engine.

Speed restraint has usually involved the use of add-on measures such as speed humps and chicanes, as commonly used to traffic-calm existing roads. In new housing developments there is the opportunity to control speeds using the minimum number of such devices, by starting from first principles in how the area is to be laid out.

Traffic-calming added as an afterthought

Tight corners and pinch points in the street encourage drivers to drive cautiously. Poundbury, Dorset

Selective street closures direct traffic to the main streets while allowing pedestrians and cyclists a full choice of routes. Canning Street, Liverpool

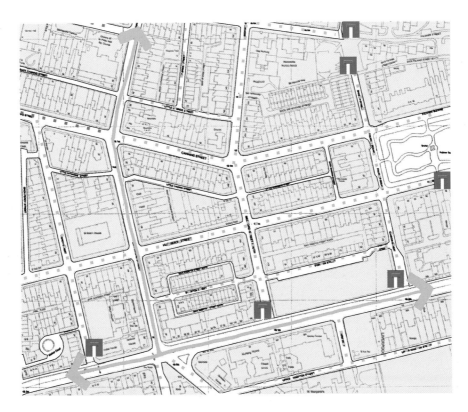

Select closures

Main route

Cycle & pedestrian routes

The lesson from countless traditional towns is that the overall arrangement of buildings and spaces, by obstructing forward vision, induces drivers to go slowly. The same effect can be achieved in new developments by using the technique known as 'tracking', as described in *Places, Streets and Movement*[3]. This method gives priority to the arrangement of buildings and spaces, with the carriageway threaded through. As well as helping create a traffic-calmed environment, tracking has two major benefits:

- it helps define the pattern of the spaces and enclosures which characterise a distinctive place;
- it allows a reduction in unsightly traffic signage and other highway clutter.

But even with the best layout based on the principle of tracking, features such as raised crossings and raised junctions may be necessary. These help indicate that the pedestrian should have priority, as well as helping break up the street layout.

Tracking is an essential tool in the placemaking process. The most comprehensive example of the use of tracking in a housing layout is at Poundbury, where it has been successfully adopted in the design since the inception of the scheme in 1990. Other more recent developments, such as Thorley Lane illustrated here, have followed the lead but with modifications.

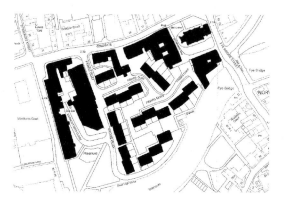

Layout of buildings and spaces has a traffic-calming effect. Friars Quay, Norwich

At both Poundbury and Thorley Lane the principle of tracking has been used to create good street enclosure and interesting spaces. At Poundbury the footpaths are laid out to follow the building line. This has a traffic-calming effect. At Thorley Lane the footpaths follow the carriageway, creating a greater emphasis on the roadspace

Poundbury

Thorley Lane

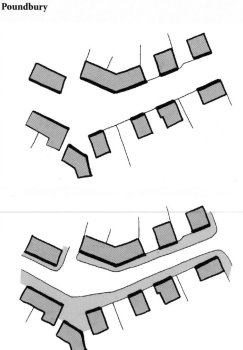

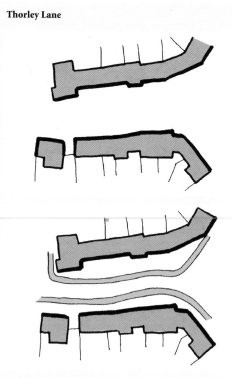

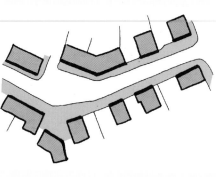

▓ **Footpath**

Servicing the home

Modern houses are more heavily serviced than their predecessors. Some of these services have a visual impact on development, especially the arrangements for refuse vehicle access.

In some places it is possible to bring refuse vehicles to the rear of the house, but generally they use the road at the front. Where that happens it is important that their requirements are met, but are not allowed to dictate the layout. In particular, it is possible to accommodate the turning space at the end of a closed-off street as part of the arrangement of buildings, rather than as a piece of severe road geometry.

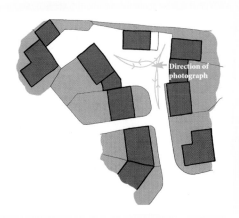

Direction of photograph

—— **Turning circle for bin lorry**

Turning places at the end of closed off streets are defined by the arrangement of buildings. Thorley Lane, Bishops Stortford

Some key points

In appraising the movement aspects of any new development, the following key points should be considered:

Streets and spaces

- Is the development based on a high quality network of streets and spaces catering for all residents and their visitors, or does it give primacy to the movement of vehicles?
- Is traffic-calming an integral part of the layout design?

Connections

- Will the development be well-connected to existing routes, and will it allow links to be made for future developments?

Travel choices

- Does the development provide for all forms of travel, including walking, cycling and public transport?
- Is the density sufficient to support an efficient bus service?

End notes:

1 Shared surface streets raise particular issues for disabled people. Further advice will be forthcoming on this issue as a result of an ongoing project being taken forward by DTLR to provide good practice guidance on catering for the needs of disabled people through the planning system.

2 Towards an Urban Renaissance: The Report of the Urban Task Force page 61.

3 See page 55.

04

Housing mix and neighbourhood

- Creating mixed communities
- Providing a range of housing opportunities
- Integrating special needs and general housing
- Supporting the community
- Some key points

Creating mixed communities

The creation of successful residential environments is about much more than visually attractive design. It is also in essence about providing opportunities for homes which respond to people's needs and providing a framework within which communities can become established and grow.

Mixed neighbourhoods of people of different ages and economic status and with different lifestyles and different levels of mobility and independence can provide a number of important community benefits. For example, they can:

- lead to a better balance of demand for community services and facilities such as schools, recreation facilities and care for elderly people;
- provide opportunities for 'lifetime communities' where people can move home without leaving a neighbourhood;
- make neighbourhoods more robust by avoiding large concentrations of housing of the same type;
- enable community self-help such as with arrangements for child care, help with shopping, the garden or during the winter freeze;
- assist community surveillance with people coming and going throughout the day and evening, as compared to the dormitory suburb which becomes deserted during the working day, making the opportunities for crime easier.

The provision of a mix of housing types and uses[1] can also contribute to the creation of more attractive residential environments by enabling a greater diversity of building forms and scales. For example:

- apartments can give scale to local centres and turn corners elegantly with continuous frontage;
- town houses can contribute to more formal compositions of avenues, circuses and squares and help frame open spaces;
- community buildings such as schools and health centres can be designed to give status to civic spaces and provide a focus for community.

The provision of a range of housing in terms of dwelling size, type and affordability as well as appropriate community facilities and services, such as open spaces, créches, daycare and health services, are all important in creating the framework within which communities can grow.

Providing a range of housing opportunities

A good mix of both housing types and sizes is important in creating a basis for a balanced community. The case studies show that even comparatively small developments can embrace a wide mix of dwelling types.

The Rolls Crescent development at Hulme demonstrates how design flair can deliver a very wide range of dwelling types within a coherent street scene. Within the scheme of 67 dwellings there are 11 different dwelling types ranging from three-storey, 5-bedroom houses to single-storey 2-bedroom units designed to be wheelchair accessible.

A range of different housing opportunities are well integrated to create a balanced community and a coherent street scene. Rolls Crescent, Hulme

Much recent housing has provided a limited range of tenure choices, often focusing on a narrow market segment or particular housing need. Even where affordable housing has been provided as part of a development, it has often been poorly integrated with homes developed for private rent or sale.

At Poundbury, more than 20% of the dwellings provided in the first phase of development are for affordable rent. These are provided mainly in small groups of between two and four dwellings which are scattered throughout the development. A key point is that in terms of building form and external appearance they are indistinguishable from the homes for private sale.

Homes for affordable rent

Small groups of houses for affordable rent scattered throughout the first phase of development at Poundbury, Dorchester

Integrating different housing types and needs can greatly enrich the quality of community life by engendering both a sense of belonging and a sense of respect for all.

However, care needs to be taken at all stages of the design process to ensure that the range of housing needs is fully understood (including taking expert advice as appropriate) and to make sure that any potential conflicts between the lifestyles of different groups are taken into account.

The successful integration of special and general needs housing can be helped by innovative design approaches which deal with the requirements of care providers in relation to the place rather than by building standard solutions.

The development of Webster's Yard, Kendal demonstrates the potential of such an approach. Here, 44 sheltered dwellings for elderly people have been designed alongside a dozen houses and apartments for sale on a narrow, sloping town centre site. The quality and richness of the development reflect the careful crafting of the scheme to fit its context and could not have been achieved through the use of standard types.

The Trowbridge Estate, London

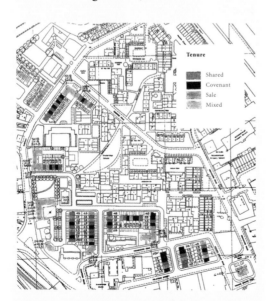

In an inner urban context, the redevelopment of the Trowbridge Estate seeks to create a wide range of housing choices. The result is a 'pepper potting' of different housing opportunities around the development.

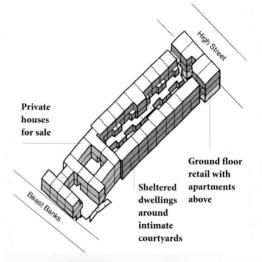

Responding to the characteristics and the needs of residents through design. Webster's Yard, Kendal

Supporting the community

The analysis of the area surrounding a site (see Chapter 2) will build up a clear picture of the existing facilities and services which residents will be able to access conveniently on foot. This is an important starting point in considering the need for new community facilities and services in an area and whether it may be appropriate and possible (in terms of site size and the availability of funding) to provide these as part of the overall development of the site.

The key point is that the provision of new facilities and services should build on and enhance the range and quality of facilities already available in the area, including residents' access to them. For example, it may well make more sense to secure improvements to the quality of an existing open space or play area close to a site rather than seeking additional provision on the site itself. Consultation with the local community can help enormously in ensuring that proposals reflect community aspirations as well as encouraging local people to take a stake in decisions about their neighbourhood.

Some activities and uses (such as late night entertainment or noisy sports or play) will be incompatible with the lifestyle aspirations of some people, but this need not necessarily require the activities to be geographically separated from dwellings. Many potential problems can be resolved through careful attention to detailed design and arrangements for long term management. For example, by taking care in:
- locating noisy activities such as play facilities for older children away from residents who may be particularly sensitive to noise;
- using the mix of different dwelling types (and lifestyles) to create buffers between quiet areas and areas of intense use;
- locating bedrooms away from noise sources.

These considerations of design and management are important because often the easy option of separating activities and uses can contribute to the creation of problem areas. For example, placing children's play areas to the rear of dwellings, or in the corner of a site where it cannot be overlooked, helps to create the conditions for nuisance and antisocial behaviour.

Open space at the heart of a community provides a sense of identity and a safe place to play. Boscombe, Bournemouth

Open spaces at the rear of dwellings have no civic value and often become a source of nuisance

Medical centre at ground floor level with apartments above. Isledon Village, Islington

With imaginative design, the provision of community facilities can not only support community development and meet needs, but also help create a focus and sense of identity for a neighbourhood. Too often inadequate attention has been paid to this potential with:

- 'a site' for a school or open space being provided as a planning requirement, rather than as an integral part of an urban design strategy;
- the facility being developed to meet the functional requirements of the user or provider without proper regard for its civic design potential.

This can result in civic buildings being dispersed around a site, rather than drawn together to create a community centre and a focus for the public transport network.

The benefits of an integrated approach to urban design are illustrated at Isledon Village, Islington, London. In this case an intensive community consultation programme helped to define priorities for the provision of community facilities and a vision of how these should be incorporated into the new residential neighbourhood.

The resulting development includes a variety of community facilities catering for a range of needs and has been successfully incorporated into the scheme. These include a medical centre at ground floor level with apartments above, a nursing home for elderly people with mental health problems and a self-built nursery school with a community room and play facilities for local children.

Some key points

In terms of providing a framework for the development of a mixed community, the following key points should be considered:

Housing mix

- Does the development provide a range of housing opportunities in terms of dwelling types, size, affordability and accessibility?
- How successfully have different types of housing been integrated with each other?

Community facilities

- Has the need for any supporting community facilities and services been considered in relation to existing patterns of provision?
- Has the provision of community facilities been considered as a part of the urban design strategy for the site?

End notes:

1 The forthcoming DTLR publication *Mixed Use Development: practice and potential* gives further consideration to the delivery of mixed use development, including housing, in town centres

05

Housing layout and urban form

- The importance of structure
- Perimeter blocks
- Other block structures
- Street widths and enclosure
- Setbacks
- Solar orientation
- Public, private and communal space
- Designing for privacy
- Creating a feeling of safety
- Accommodating parking
- Some key points

The importance of structure

This chapter is concerned with the structure of the residential environment: the arrangement and inter-relationships of streets, homes, gardens and places for leisure and parking.

Getting the structure of a residential environment right is fundamental to the success of any area. Many of the best residential environments (in metropolitan, urban, suburban and village settings) display a very clearly defined and coherent urban structure. This is characterised by a framework of inter-connected routes which define 'blocks' of housing, open spaces and other uses. The resulting structure of blocks can be viewed at different levels. For example, large neighbourhood blocks are defined by principal movement routes. These are then divided by a network of local streets to define a series of street blocks.

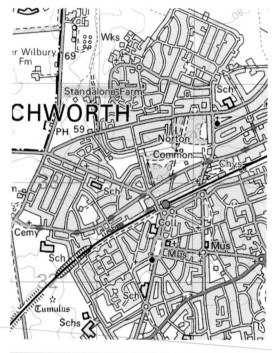

Movement routes define blocks of housing, open space and other uses. Letchworth Garden Suburb, Hertfordshire

The layout of housing within these street blocks can take a wide variety of forms including, for example, streets, squares, courts, mews, circuses or avenues. The scale is intimate, grand or somewhere in between. The fact that there is a unit which is larger than the individual home but smaller than the district helps to contribute both to a sense of scale and to a sense of belonging and community.

It is important to appreciate that some of our most attractive and enduring residential environments have the simplest of structures and are often nothing more than a regular pattern of rectangular blocks. Their visual quality comes not from the two-dimensional layout, but from the mix of activities and from the quality in detailing of the buildings, the landscape and the interfaces between these elements. The block structure works in terms of providing direct and convenient routes for movement, in making efficient use of land and in providing a tried and tested framework around which a quality place can be crafted.

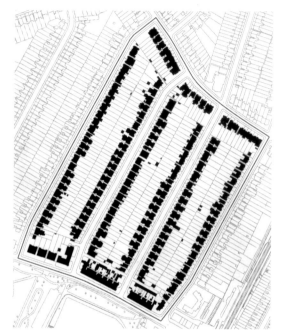

Some of the most attractive and enduring residential environments have the simplest of structures. In this classic street block structure, houses face the street, gardens run end-to-end and cars are mainly parked on the street. The sense of quality comes from the detailed design of the buildings, the corners and boundary treatments and from the mature landscape. Fox Lane, Enfield

C 1950 – 2000

C 1900 – 1950

C 1800 – 1900

A block structure defined by a network of inter-connected movement routes has been a predominant form of housing layout for centuries. Only relatively recently have structures created primarily for the car resulted in formless residential environments characterised by a dead-end road system of 'loops and lollipops'

Many recently developed areas lack any sense of coherent urban structure. In particular, many suffer from layouts which:

- are difficult to understand and to move around within;
- create left over and ill-defined spaces;
- result in a haphazard arrangement of dwellings, with houses turning their backs and blank facades towards important routes and spaces;
- make walking and cycling inconvenient because of an introverted and dead-end movement framework.

In many cases these shortcomings reflect the rigid application of highway engineering standards in terms of road hierarchies, junction separation distances, sight lines and turning radii for service vehicles. The result is often a sense of sprawl and formlessness and development which contradicts some of the key principles of urban design.

Another characteristic of many residential environments which have failed the test of time is that they have been based on experimental or convoluted layouts. Often this has resulted in a development performing very well in terms of one or two objectives, but very poorly in other important respects.

This does not mean that future housing should simply copy the structure of historic environments. Requirements have changed, not least in terms of accommodating the car, and there are many aspects of historic practice which can be improved upon.

The key point is that the structure of the residential environment needs to be created with a broad range of objectives in mind and in this respect there is much to learn from both contemporary and historic practice. The focus of this chapter is on drawing out these transferable lessons.

A coherent block structure is not just a feature of historic practice. It also forms the basis of a number of recent schemes which have also satisfied the requirements for servicing and road safety. Isledon Village, Islington

Perimeter blocks

The perimeter block structure has proved to be robust over time. In particular, perimeter blocks can provide for:
- good connections to the surrounding area (see Chapter 3);
- efficient use of land;
- a clear distinction between the public and private realms;
- a legible environment;
- good natural surveillance of the street with windows and doors facing outwards.

Forms of perimeter blocks

The perimeter block can take a wide variety of forms including:
- regular rectangular or square blocks based on a grid;
- concentric grids designed to promote access to local centres or public transport routes;
- irregular layouts with a more 'organic' character.

The case studies show that these basic forms are not mutually exclusive. Poundbury, for instance, combines an organic character with a concentric grid layout focused on the local centre.

Different forms of perimeter block can impart different characters to the streetscape. Compare, for example, the formal character of Jesmond, Newcastle with its uniform street widths and building heights, with the more intimate character of Thorley Lane, Bishops Stortford and its more variable building line. However, despite these differences of character, the underlying benefits of the perimeter block remain.

Regular – almost a 'grid iron' – layout of blocks in a suburban context. Jesmond, Newcastle

Concentric blocks arranged to promote access to a local centre. Poundbury, Dorchester

An irregular block structure providing an 'organic' and intimate character. Thorley Lane, Bishops Stortford

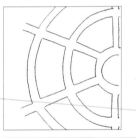

Regular blocks

Jesmond, Newcastle

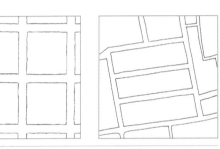

Concentric blocks

Poundbury, Dorchester

Irregular blocks

Thorley Lane, Bishops Stortford

The arrangement of dwellings within the block structure

A characteristic of perimeter blocks is that dwellings face outwards towards the edge of the block and the public realm and there is a continuity in the relationships between the fronts and backs of dwellings.

The arrangement of dwellings within the block structure and their relationship to the street and to other building elements are influenced by the plan form of the dwellings themselves (for example, wide frontage/shallow plan; narrow frontage/deep plan; or square plan). The orientation of windows is also an important consideration, particularly in relation to the treatment of block corners.

Shallow and square plan dwellings provide greater opportunities to create varied street layouts and are much better suited to informal 'organic' layouts than deep plan dwellings. Both Thorley Lane, Bishops Stortford and Poundbury, Dorchester show how a continuous but varied building line can be created with a mix of dwelling frontages, garden and garage walls.

By contrast, the historic case study areas (Canning Street, Jesmond and Stanstead) show how narrow-frontage, deep plan forms can be utilised in predominantly straight runs of terraces with continuous building frontages to provide a very land-efficient layout in terms of both development density and the ratio of dwellings to street length.

Different dwelling plans

Houses

Narrow frontage, deep plan with through aspect

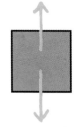

Square plan with through aspect

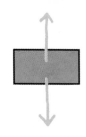

Wide frontage, shallow plan with through aspect

Wide frontage, shallow plan with single aspect

Apartments

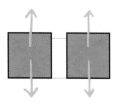

Square plan with through aspect

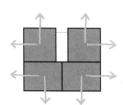

Square plan with corner aspect

A mix of square and shallow plan dwellings provides a continuous street frontage. Rolls Crescent, Manchester

Narrow frontage, deep plan dwellings provide generous internal space and use land efficiently. Stanstead Road, Lewisham

Designing for corners

The treatment of corners requires careful consideration, particularly where perimeter blocks incorporate sharp corners. The key design issues include:

- maintaining a continuity of frontage and visual surveillance;
- securing a direct relationship between habitable rooms and gardens;
- ensuring privacy between habitable rooms within the corner;
- allowing light penetration to garden space and habitable rooms;
- articulating prominent junctions and nodal points.

The case studies illustrate a range of different approaches to these issues with varying levels of success. Stanstead Road, Lewisham and, to a lesser extent, Jesmond, Newcastle highlight a common shortcoming in Victorian housing with limited or no frontage along the short end of the block, thus creating an area that is not overlooked and which can become a focus for nuisance and vandalism.

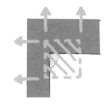

Unusable space in the corner   **Creating space in the corner**

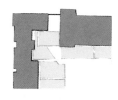

Fitting in the gardens   **Relating gardens to habitable rooms**

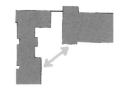

Light penetration to the corner   **Ensuring privacy**

Blank gable ends can encourage graffiti and nuisance

The more recent case studies show how these issues can be addressed through careful design. At Rolls Crescent, Hulme three-storey houses give prominence to the corners, and the use of both square and shallow plan dwellings allows the corners to be turned with continuous frontage and aspect to the street, as well as allowing light penetration to the windows of habitable rooms within the corner.

Rolls Crescent also succeeds in resolving the relationship between principal habitable rooms and private garden space within the corner. At Greenland Passage, Southwark this issue is addressed by incorporating into the corners single aspect apartments without private gardens.

Family houses with gardens on a corner. Rolls Cresent, Hulme

Block dimensions

There are no hard and fast rules in terms of the optimum dimensions of a perimeter block; indeed a variety of different block lengths is important in adding richness to a neighbourhood. The case studies highlight a number of key considerations including:

- balancing land efficiency with the need to provide convenient pedestrian routes through an area and to important local facilities;
- traffic management in terms of controlling vehicle speeds and discouraging rat-running (see Chapter 3);
- the spatial needs of activities which are to be accommodated within the block.

The historic 'long grid' often achieved land efficiency at the expense of convenient pedestrian movement and this explains why long residential blocks were often orientated along the main pedestrian desire lines. The Rolls Crescent scheme at Hulme represents the opposite extreme with very short (70 x 80 metres) square blocks providing a very high degree of pedestrian permeability through the area. Between these two extremes, a block length of between 100 and 150 metres would represent a general rule-of-thumb.

Decisions about the use of space within the block are also a significant factor in determining appropriate block dimensions. At Rolls Crescent, for example, the objective to provide a secure sitting out and play area for use by immediate neighbours has resulted in a small and intimate urban block. By contrast, at Thorley Lane, Bishops Stortford and Poundbury, Dorchester the decision to accommodate car parking *within* the block has resulted in much larger blocks.

Rolls Crescent, Hulme

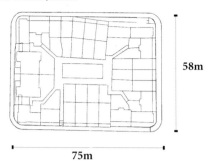

Thorley Lane, Bishops Stortford

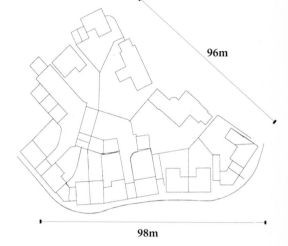

Poundbury, Dorchester

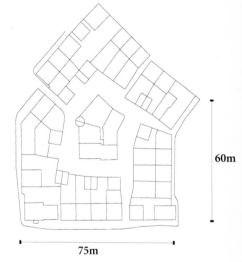

Stanstead, Lewisham

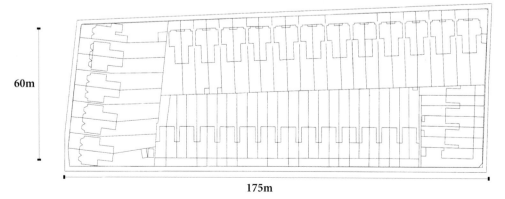

Access to back of block areas

A key consideration in the design of residential blocks is the degree of public access provided to areas within the block. It is here that some of the significant choices and trade-offs need to be made between competing objectives. Principal among these is the tension between the arrangements for servicing (including car parking) and the security of dwellings and garden areas.

Servicing dwellings from within the block (such as at Jesmond, Poundbury and Thorley Lane) can improve the appearance of the streetscape in terms of car parking and refuse collection and enable residents to have access to the rear of gardens. However, these advantages need to be carefully balanced against other concerns. In particular:

- rear servicing can undermine the security of dwellings by allowing strangers access to the rear of dwellings;
- without very careful attention to detailed design, rear parking courts and alleyways can become unpleasant and even hostile places;
- rear courtyard parking can reduce the area available for back gardens and the coming and going of cars can detract from the tranquility of garden areas.

The design of Poundbury successfully overcomes some of these concerns by incorporating dwellings into the rear courtyards to provide surveillance and to create an attractive public space. Yet care needs to be taken in replicating this model, both in ensuring that the design principles are carried through as rigorously as at Poundbury, Dorchester and in taking account of the density of development and the character of the surrounding area.

The Stanstead Road, Lewisham and Rolls Crescent, Hulme case study areas both achieve complete enclosure of the back of block area. This helps to make the rear of dwellings secure and the arrangement of rear garden to rear garden (as at Stanstead) provides the opportunity for substantial landscaped areas within the block. However, it requires dwellings to be serviced from the front and cars to be parked on the street. A particular issue in respect of terraced houses can be the need to carry garden equipment and waste through the house, unless a shared and gated front access to back yards and gardens is provided. The same point applies to building maintenance and to any future building work at the back of the house.

Enclosed backs give security to the rear of dwellings and provide space for more generous gardens, but parking and servicing must be accommodated in the front. Stanstead Road, Lewisham

Rear service alleys provide convenient access to rear gardens and can remove bin storage and clutter from the street. However, they raise serious issues in terms of safety and security. Here bins in the alley also provide a platform for burglars to scale the rear wall and gain access to the back of the home. Jesmond, Newcastle

Parking in courts within the block can improve the quality of the street scene, but this can have implications in terms of the size, security and tranquility of gardens. Thorley Lane, Bishops Stortford

Placing dwellings within the parking courts can help to improve natural surveillance. Here the design creates a public space which has cars parked in it, rather than a car park. Poundbury, Dorchester

Extent of public access

Housing layout and urban form

Other block structures

Until recently, perimeter blocks were the most common and robust form of housing layout, but there are situations where a different form of layout is appropriate. These can include constrained sites or those where a 'setpiece' development is required, such as one overlooking an important civic space.

Equally, perimeter blocks can accommodate a variety of layout forms within them. Specifically, cul-de-sac forms can work very well within a wider block structure. This can add interest and diversity as well as making good use of backland areas within large development blocks.

Highsett, Cambridge shows how a secluded and intimate residential area with good pedestrian links into the surrounding area can be created within a larger block. Where such opportunities are taken it is important that the scale and massing of development within the block respect that of the buildings forming the main block and take account of the existing orientation of fronts and backs.

Unwin and Parker's plan for Letchworth (1907), based on a perimeter block structure but with enclosed layouts within larger blocks and buildings on special sites

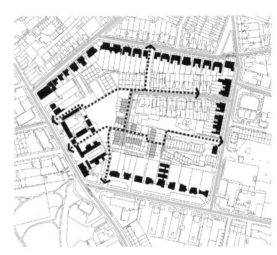

■ Buildings forming wider urban block
▨ Third Phase of development at Highsett enclosed by wider block
···> Pedestrian routes

Enclosed housing layout relying on a wider block structure which maintains continuity of frontage to the principal routes around the block, Highsett, Cambridge

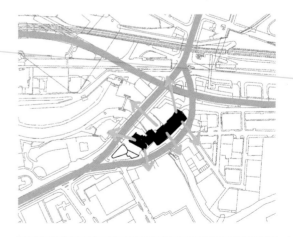

A pavilion building is 'civic' on all sides. Here the attributes of the perimeter block form are condensed into a single building. Deansgate Quay, Manchester

'Local planning
authorities should adopt
policies which . . . focus
on the quality of the
places and living
environments being
created and give priority
to the needs of
pedestrians rather than
the movement and
parking of vehicles.'

*PPG3: Housing
paragraph 56*

Street widths and enclosure

Designing residential streets around the functional
requirements of cars, service vehicles and utilities,
with inadequate attention being paid to other
important amenity requirements, has been one of
the greatest failings of much recent development.
In comparison to the best historic residential
environments, the consequences have included:

- a loss of local identity through the widespread
  application of the same standards;
- an incoherent relationship of dwellings to the
  street and to each other;
- a lack of any sense of enclosure;
- the loss of front garden areas to hardstandings
  for off–street car parking;
- the loss of boundary treatments, such as walls
  and well-managed hedges, which define public
  and private space and articulate the boundaries
  between dwellings;
- often an absence of street trees.

**This street has a very good sense of enclosure. Street width
and building heights are well related and the tall building at
the end of the street terminates the view. Greenland Passage,
Southwark**

There are no hard and fast rules. Indeed the case
studies show that streets can work at widths as
varied as nine metres (Rolls Crescent, Hulme) and
24 metres (Canning Street, Liverpool). What is
important is that the space between the buildings
is considered in relation to the scale of dwellings
and the activities taking place in the street. For
example, Canning Street works well with a very
wide separation because the street is framed by
12 -14 metre high buildings. In other cases
landscaping can help create a sense of enclosure
where wider spacing is required between dwellings,
such as along principal movement routes.

It follows from this that the design of streets needs
to be tailored to the particular needs of the place
and its physical and social context and considered
in three dimensions.

Varying ratios of street width to building height

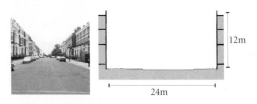

1:2 ratio, Canning Street, Liverpool

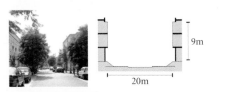

1:2.2 ratio, Isledon Village, Islington

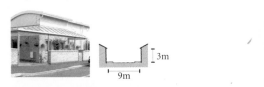

1:3 ratio, Halston Street, Hulme

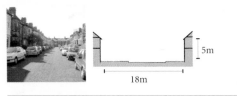

1:3.6 ratio, Cavendish Place, Jesmond

In looking at the degree of enclosure achieved
in the case study areas, it is also important to
remember that the historic case study areas feature
higher floor-to-ceiling heights than would be the
norm today. Hence, creating the same sense of
enclosure with the same number of building-
storeys would require a reduced separation
distance between facing dwellings, for example as
at Poundbury, Thorley Lane and Rolls Crescent.
By contrast, at Isledon Road, monopitch roofs
have been used to lend a larger scale to the
street elevations.

Setbacks

The setback of dwellings from the street is a key consideration in terms of:
- defining the character of the street;
- determining the degree of privacy given to ground floor rooms;
- accommodating storage and service requirements at the front of the dwelling.

It is no exaggeration to say that the success or failure of a street can often depend on the design of a one or two metre setback between the dwelling and the footway.

Where dwellings are serviced from the rear, such as at Poundbury, Thorley Lane and Friars Quay, dwellings can be pushed forward to the 'back of footway' with no or very little setback to create a very intimate environment without compromising either the storage space for bins and utilities or ease of access by service vehicles. Where this is done, careful consideration needs to be given to the design of front door and threshold areas, particularly in relation to security. At Poundbury the use of recessed porches helps to enhance the threshold to the dwelling.

The other case studies show that even a very modest setback of a metre or so can be sufficient to accommodate bin and cycle storage and provide privacy to front rooms, while a setback of three to five metres can provide for a small front garden. Issues of detailed design in relation to setbacks and thresholds are considered further in Chapter 7.

A zero setback. Poundbury, Dorchester

A minimal (1-2 metre) setback. Thorley Lane, Bishops Stortford

A small front garden (within a 3 – 5 metre setback) provides privacy and a buffer to the street. Stanstead Road, Lewisham

A larger front garden (within a 5 – 7 metre setback) provides a landscape structure and setting for the house. Jesmond, Newcastle

Housing layout and urban form

Solar orientation

The orientation of dwellings in relation to the sun is important, not only in relation to the arrangement of gardens and principal habitable rooms (see Chapter 6), but also in influencing the potential to reduce energy requirements within the home. For example, daylighting reduces the need for artificial lighting and passive solar gain reduces the need for internal space heating. Emerging technologies involving the use of photovoltaic cells can convert solar radiation into electricity, while solar panels can provide a source of hot water for washing and heating.

The optimum orientation in terms of maximising solar potential is for dwellings to face southwards, with streets arranged in an east-west pattern and with a generous separation between dwellings to provide for full solar access. However, strict adherence to these principles can result in trade-offs against other planning and urban design objectives. For example:

- the orientation of the street pattern also needs to be considered in relation to pedestrian desire lines and connections to existing places and routes;
- orientating all dwellings towards the south can undermine the relationships between the fronts and backs of dwellings and reduce natural surveillance of the street;
- very wide spacing between dwellings can result in an inefficient use of land and weaken a sense of street enclosure.

In fact, with careful orientation of streets and the arrangement of dwellings within the block structure, it is possible to provide good opportunities for solar gain and daylight penetration to habitable rooms, while at the same time addressing other key principles of good urban design. Once again, design decisions need to be made in the round to reach a considered balance between competing design objectives.

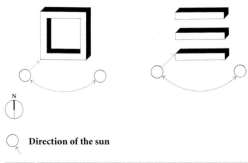

 **Direction of the sun**

Standard perimeter block creates areas of overshadowing

South-facing terraces maximise solar gain but can compromise other design objectives

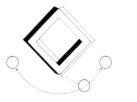

Orientating blocks to the sun's path reduces overshadowed areas within the block

Breaks in the building form or reduced storey heights increase solar penetration of the block

Denser urban apartment blocks require careful consideration to ensure good solar penetration to the interior of the block. Here a break in the building block at the third storey allows good sunlight penetration to an attractive communal space. Narrow Street, Tower Hamlets, London.

Public, private and communal space

Most residential environments comprise a mix of, public, private and communal spaces. It is important that the role of each space is clear and that the boundaries between different types of space are clearly defined. Left-over space is wasted space which in time is likely to become a source of nuisance.

Rigid adherence to highway design standards, in this case sight lines between front driveways and the street, undermines the quality and utility of front gardens and blurs the distinction between the public realm of the street and the private realm of the dwelling. Residents or visitors still find it more convenient to park on the street despite generous off- street parking provision

Here cars are parked on the street and public and private space is clearly defined by walls, hedges and gates. Valley Drive, Harrogate

Public open space is potentially one of a community's greatest assets. The best open spaces are those which not only cater safely for play, exercise and relaxation, but which also provide an area with a sense of identity and community. In many cases this will involve drawing the open space to the heart of the neighbourhood to create an important structural element within the overall urban design strategy (see Chapter 4).

Open space can bring character and quality to a neighbourhood and provide residents with a pleasant outlook. Park Mews, Hulme

Where communal space is provided as internal gardens or courtyards in higher density housing, care needs to be taken to protect privacy and amenity to the rear of ground floor dwellings. This is successfully achieved in parts of Greenland Passage where the ground floor of townhouses and apartments opens into a small patio area, which provides a buffer to the attractive communal garden beyond.

The addition of planting helps to define the boundary between private and communal space and creates a degree of privacy for private patios. Greenland Passage, Southwark.

Designing for privacy

Privacy is an important design objective in ensuring that residents feel at ease within their home. It is also an area where general planning standards prescribing minimum separation distances between habitable rooms can frustrate the creation of attractive residential environments by denying the ability to provide privacy through careful design.

Design can help create privacy in a number of ways:
- street design can influence the relationship between facing dwellings. A varied building line (such as at Thorley Lane, Bishops Stortford and Poundbury, Dorchester) can create oblique views, allowing the fronts of dwellings to be brought closer together than where facing views are direct, such as at Jesmond;
- rooms needing less privacy, such as living rooms and kitchens, can face the street with bedrooms and bathrooms located towards more private parts of the home;
- windows can be designed in relation to the function of the room: generous windows for living rooms overlooking the street or a garden; frosted windows for bathrooms; and smaller windows for bedrooms. Bay windows provide oblique views down a street;
- the careful orientation of primary and secondary windows can enable dwellings to be drawn close together while still providing surveillance of the public realm;
- screening and landscaping can limit overlooking between facing rear windows.

Thus, while there are well established rules of thumb (such as a minimum 'back-to-back' distance of 20 metres), these need to be applied flexibly in relation to the specific context and in the recognition that the objective of privacy can often be better secured through careful design rather than by physical separation alone.

Smaller kitchen windows balance the need for surveillance with privacy. Isledon Road, Islington

A varied building line creates oblique views across the street. Thorley Lane, Bishops Stortford

A failure to consider the need for privacy can result in curtains and blinds being permanently drawn

Creating a feeling of safety

Design has a crucial role to play in delivering and creating a sense of safety and security. A key issue is that of natural surveillance. Streets which are well overlooked and which have activity in them throughout the day and evening benefit from the presence and surveillance of residents and visitors.

Good planning and design can help by ensuring that:
- dwellings fronting the street have their principal entrance on to it;
- windows are designed to maximise overlooking of the street;
- continuity of frontage and aspect is maintained on corners;
- blank facades and areas which are not overlooked are avoided;
- the mix of dwelling types and sizes encourages activity in the street throughout the day and evening (see Chapter 4 on dwelling mix and neighbourhood).

Designing for safety and security should not be separated from consideration of details such as those addressed by *Secured by Design* and issues of long-term management; the latter being particularly important in relation to higher density apartment development. Considerations of the number of dwellings to be served by a common entrance and the introduction of concierge schemes can often prove fundamental to the ultimate success of a place.

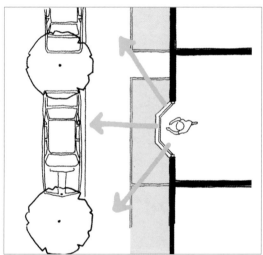

The archetypal 'safe street'. Windows overlook it, doors open onto it, enabling people to see and be seen. Ideally, shrubbery would be managed to a height which allows privacy but still provides for natural surveillance. Jesmond, Newcastle

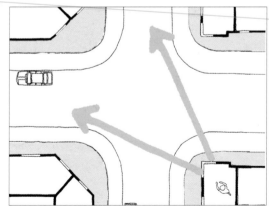

Corner windows can provide views in several directions. Rolls Crescent, Hulme

Accommodating parking

Where and how cars are parked are crucial to the quality of housing development and to the choices people make in how they travel. The level of parking provision and its location are both equally important. Car owners want to be able to park near their home and to be able to see their car. In meeting these aspirations the typical result is a car-dominated environment with 'car platforms' in front of houses or integral garages facing the street.

Cars dominating the housing frontage

This has a number of negative consequences including:

- eliminating front garden space and the opportunities for landscape and planting;
- blurring the distinction between public and private space by preventing traditional boundary treatments;
- removing the opportunity to park on the street;
- introducing potential conflicts between pedestrians and cars which have to cross the footway to park.

In addition, dedicating car parking spaces to individual dwellings does not provide the same flexibility towards variations in car ownership between households as communal arrangements do.

Instead of the dominance of cars parked in front of houses, there are often opportunities to use a combination of dedicated and communal parking, especially in developments where secure communal provision can be made an integral part of the overall site layout. The particular context and requirements of a site can help to furnish an appropriate solution.

As a guide to establishing parking policies that support sustainable development, PPG3 points to an upper threshold of 1.5 spaces per dwelling on average. It is to be expected that, with a sustainable approach to parking, local authorities will revise their parking standards to allow for significantly lower levels of parking than have been the case recently, particularly for developments:

- in locations where services are readily accessible by walking, cycling or public transport;
- which provide housing where the demand for parking is likely to be less than for family housing;
- involving conversions where off-street parking is less likely to be successfully designed into the scheme.

Whatever format of parking is chosen, special account needs to be taken of those with restricted mobility, espcially in getting in and out of parked cars and approaching the front door of a house.

On-street parking

Most traditional terraced housing in many towns throughout the country has adjusted well to the advent of the car. Streets in inner suburbs, such as Jesmond, although not designed for the car, show that on-street parking can work. It is convenient, well overlooked from surrounding houses and is extremely efficient, both in terms of the amount of space required for parking and in providing for variations in car ownership between households. On-street parking can also have a traffic-calming effect, helps to separate pedestrians from other traffic and provides the opportunity to include boundary treatment landscaping for dwellings.

On-street parking in a traditional street. Jesmond, Newcastle

In new developments (or the upgrading of existing areas) there is much to be said for on-street parking, but with the 'line of steel' interrupted at intervals.

On-street parking bays can be incorporated into the overall width of the street, demarcated by paving, trees and planting. There are two main types:

- *Parallel parking* against the kerb. The example illustrated is of streets with good surveillance from neighbouring houses;
- *Angled parking bays*. These allow a greater parking capacity than parallel parking, but because of the danger from reversing vehicles, they are only suitable for streets with low traffic speeds.

Parallel parking against the curb can have a traffic-calming effect. Canning Street, Liverpool

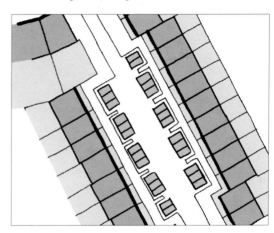

Right-angled parking bays (see also photograph below). Isledon Village, Islington

Right-angled and parallel parking. In this arrangement there is one space per dwelling and the parking bays are broken up by tree planting. Isledon Village, Islington.

Housing layout and urban form

Courtyard parking

Communal parking in courtyards has gained a bad reputation because of inadequately designed parking courts from the 1960s and 1970s, usually located away from housing and therefore lacking surveillance.

But more recently it has been shown that secure rear courtyards can be a useful addition to dedicated spaces in front of dwellings. Courtyards which work well exhibit three main characteristics:

- they are not car parks but places which have parking in them;
- they are overlooked by adjoining houses, or by buildings entered from the parking area;
- they normally include at most ten parking spaces. If there are more spaces the courtyard layout should be broken up.

The courtyard will usually be located at the centre of a street block, designed as an integral part of the development. Ideally, it will have more than one access point, forming a route across the block, although in some locations concerns about security may preclude that arrangement.

The entrance to a rear courtyard, between buildings or through an archway, needs to respect the street frontage. Over wide openings are unnecessary if serving ten spaces or fewer, and they may damage the continuity of the street.

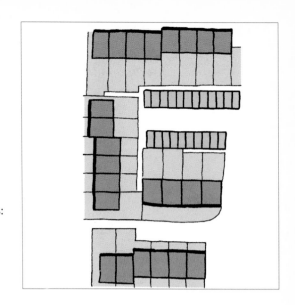

A typical 1970s development, with parking totally segregated from housing and not overlooked

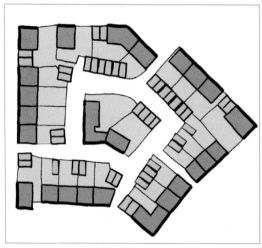

This arrangement of buildings creates a well overlooked space. Through routes increase natural surveillance from passing pedestrians. Poundbury, Dorchester

Houses within the rear courtyard provide natural surveillance. Poundbury, Dorchester

Narrow entrance arch to a rear courtyard. Black Notley, Essex.

A courtyard formed by the arrangement of buildings. Here there is no through route for pedestrians. Thorley Lane, Bishops Stortford

In–curtilage parking

Various arrangements can help mitigate the effect of parking within the building curtilage. The simplest of these is to locate the garage or carport alongside the house, set back from the building line. Many parts of Thorley Lane, Bishops Stortford show what can be gained from such a configuration. Alternatively, in some locations, the garage can be concealed as part of a boundary wall.

Basement and undercroft parking

The success of an infill development such as Webster's Yard, Kendal depends upon the use of basement parking, without which the scheme would not have been viable. Apart from the financial equation, the advantage of putting cars underground is that it preserves the street frontage. But, as with courtyard parking, much depends on the location and design of the entrance. Webster's Yard provides a clever example of concealment.

Car parking structures have a rigid geometry based on the dimensions of a parking bay, but this should not be allowed to dictate the shape of the building above.

Car clubs

Car clubs eliminate the need to own a car by allowing residents to hire vehicles as and when they need them. People wanting to use the club simply pay a small annual fee. The vehicle is then charged by the time hired and the distance driven, the operator covering insurance and maintenance costs.

Although car clubs are common in other European countries, none of the case studies had one in operation or proposed. In terms of housing layout, a successful car club offers the prospect of a development with much reduced parking provision and thus, in some cases, significantly higher densities.

Town houses with integral garages. Ingress Park, Greenhithe

View of New Inn Road, leading to basement car park at the end of the street. The treatment of the car park entrance preserves the street frontage. Webster's Yard, Kendal

This underground car park is well lit and has several pedestrian access points. Webster's Yard, Kendal

Cycle storage

One great advantage of cycling is that it is door-to-door, but the problem of where to keep a bicycle is often a deterrent to using this form of transport. The wide hallways of 19th century houses can accommodate one or two bicycles, but the tighter spaces of much recent housing militate against that solution. Storing cycles on a wall rack is one alternative or, more convenient still, the provision of an enclosed ground floor space for cycles: that space could also be used for a pram, buggy, wheelchair or electric mobility scooter.

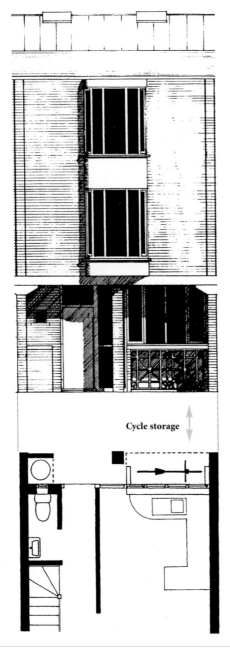

Cycle storage

The inclusion of convenient but secure cycle storage at the front of dwellings, particularly terraced housing, requires very careful design. In this example, cycle storage is provided in a recessed space below the kitchen window

In terms of creating a robust structure for the residential environment, the following key points need to be considered:

Structure

- How does the development address the need for structure? By following a perimeter block form, by working within a larger block structure or as a pavilion building responding to its setting?

Movement

- Is the block structure consistent with the objectives of the movement framework (see Chapter 3) in terms of desire lines to local centres, public transport and other facilities?

Security

- Are streets, parking areas, open spaces and play areas overlooked by dwellings?
- Are the back of block areas secure? If publicly accessible, what measures have been taken to reduce the opportunities for antisocial behaviour?

Corners

- Where perimeter blocks take a rectangular form, how have corner issues been resolved?
- Is continuity of aspect maintained? How are issues of light, privacy and access to garden space resolved within the corner?

Parking

- Do the requirements for car parking and its layout on site undermine the environmental quality of the scheme?

Open Space

- Have public open spaces helped to shape the urban design strategy for the site?
- How do dwellings relate to open space in terms of their frontage and scale?

Space in and around the home

- Thinking about space in and around the home
- Density and space
- Relating indoor and outdoor space
- Flexibility, adaptability and change
- Innovation
- Some key points

Thinking about space in and around the home

The case studies include examples of how the planning of internal space integrally with external space can produce and enrich the sense of quality and distinct identity both within the dwelling and of the neighbourhood as a whole. Equally, when these relationships between internal and external spaces are not given adequate consideration, characteristics which undermine the overall quality of the development can emerge, for example:

- living rooms lacking privacy;
- external spaces without surveillance;
- inadequate treatment of threshold areas;
- lost opportunities to benefit from orientation and views.

The lack of distinctiveness and quality which characterises so many modern housing schemes can often be attributed to the design of layout forms and the application of standard housing types in a manner which fails to consider the relationships between internal and external spaces.

This chapter is not intended to be a guide to internal space planning or standards (because pointers can be found in a number of existing publications[1]) but aims instead to stimulate thinking about the issues involved. The need for this thinking also arises in relation to other factors, including:

- greater interest in flexible internal space, as exemplified by loft developments and live/work units;
- recognition of the benefits of housing which can adapt to the changing requirements of residents;
- greater emphasis on orientation to low energy solutions.

Density and space

It is a common misunderstanding that higher housing densities need to result in lower standards of space around and within the home. While large detached houses will tend to be more spacious than town centre apartments, the case studies suggest that it is possible to provide generous living space and, at the same time, achieve higher development densities.

The case study developments completed within the last decade (for example, at: Thorley Lane, Bishops Stortford; Rolls Crescent, Hulme; Greenland Passage, Southwark; Poundbury, Dorchester; and Deansgate Quay, Manchester) provide space standards which match or better those commonly found in the private sector, or those currently recommended for public sector development[2].

Spacious town houses arranged on four floors, close to Norwich City Centre. This scheme achieves a net density of 34 dwellings per hectare. Friars Quay, Norwich

These Victorian town houses (as originally built) provide a density of 41 dwellings per hectare while still achieving a generous amount of internal space by today's standards. Canning Street, Liverpool

Generously-sized back gardens provide space for children's play and ecology. In this case a mix of three and five bedroom houses was developed at a density of 31 dwellings per hectare. Stanstead Road, Lewisham

The earlier and historic case study areas such as: Canning Street, Liverpool, Jesmond, Newcastle, and Stanstead Road, Lewisham also provide space standards which would be considered generous by today's norms at densities in the range of 30 to 50 dwellings per hectare and above.

A key factor in making this possible is the efficient provision of space for vehicle movement and car parking. The design principles relating to these issues are considered in more detail in Chapters 3 and 5.

Whatever the scale of the dwelling or form of development, maximising utility and creating a sense of space are likely to depend upon such factors as:

- the potential for daylight penetration;
- the relationship to outdoor space, whether that is provided by a balcony, garden, street or park;
- the ability to provide multi-use rather than single-use spaces;
- the efficiency of planning internal circulation and locating kitchens, utility rooms, toilets and bathrooms.

The advantages and disadvantages of the 'wet core' uses (for example, kitchens, bathrooms and utility rooms) being to the front, to the rear or in the centre of the dwelling need to be carefully considered in terms of functionality, lighting and visual impact. Ground floor street side windows generally need to be small and elevated. Large 'picture' windows on the street side of the house will tend to result in a public facade dominated by drawn blinds and curtains, with a loss of natural light to the dwelling and a loss of surveillance of the street.

It is important to analyse the relationship between the block size and frontage width in relation to internal and external space issues. The potential frequently exists to explore housing and apartment forms which use well planned and natural lighting devices to create quality solutions for deep-plan and narrow-frontage dwellings. Equally, the use of either single or double aspect apartments needs particular attention in relation to the quality of space to be enjoyed. Promising opportunities to enhance the quality of external and internal space tend to emerge at corners and street block ends.

Here the planning and use of internal space are well related to external space. Millennium Village, Greenwich

Multi-use space linking hall, kitchen, dining and living areas. Millennium Village, Greenwich

Compact circulation and kitchen space planning maximise living space. Prince of Wales Road, London

Potential for daylight penetration fully exploited through orientation, glazing, with supporting kitchen, bathroom and circulation space located away from the main elevations. St Mary's Square, Bury St Edmonds

Relating indoor and outdoor space

In seeking to relate indoor and outdoor space, the starting point needs to be an analysis of orientation and potential sources of light and views. Rooflights, open stairwells, mezzanine sections, varying ceiling heights, or steps and corners in the plan, can all help to bring daylight into the core of the dwellings.

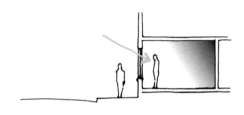

The consequence of failing to consider the relationships between outdoor and indoor space. Here car parking on a raised deck compromises the privacy (and potentially the security) of first floor apartments resulting in permanently drawn blinds. Deansgate Quay, Manchester

A mezzanine level exploits light for two levels of habitable space. Homes for Change, Hulme

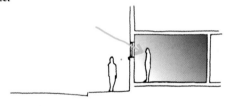

Large windows provide good daylight penetration, but also create a feeling of vulnerability with little privacy from the street

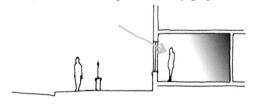

Small windows provide a greater feeling of security in the home, but also reduce the potential for daylight penetration

As well as this 'inside-to-outside' analysis, an 'outside-to-inside' analysis is also desirable. How will the street impact on the dwelling in terms of its privacy and security, light and sunlight and the definition of the public realm and the private external and internal space? How will street planting affect the dwelling and what factors need to be considered in defining the scale, form and treatment of the 'threshold space' and windows?

Large windows together with small garden setbacks can provide a solution. The use of this room is a further consideration, because kitchens and living rooms have different functional and privacy requirements

A successful balance between an active street frontage and privacy can be aided by making the ground floor level significantly higher than the pavement level. However, this poses difficulties for wheelchair access, and carefully considered solutions are needed. These may involve well designed ramps, level rear access at a higher level, or well tailored solutions to specific circumstances. Some developments have addressed the issues through the street-side ground floor being given over to the 'front' door, lobby, storage and parking space.

This wheelchair ramp has blurred the distinction between public and private space with the unintended consequence of providing a place for children to cycle and skateboard, causing nuisance to residents. Rolls Crescent, Hulme

External space to the rear requires similar analysis, whether this is private, communal or a mix of both. At ground floor level, the best solutions will provide a sharing of space, from the garden into the house and from the house into the garden, allowing for different patterns of living during the summer and winter months. Above this, the potential for balconies and roof gardens, both projected and recessed, should be explored. A key consideration is that balconies should be useable and not merely decorative. This raises specific issues, not only about size but also involves thinking about orientation, views, the circulation patterns of the internal space, massing forms such as stepped structures as well as construction methods.

In the design of any urban housing block, the optimum internal planning of each unit is likely to vary according to which side of the street the unit faces. For example, a north or east-facing kitchen facing the street has merit in terms of an active frontage, ease of access for deliveries, comfort in use and goes hand in hand with the potential for solar gain to the living and other habitable rooms on the south and west sides.

Conversely, on the opposite side of the street, living rooms, deeper gardens and balconies facing the street may be appropriate, with the 'wet core' of the house to the rear. Longer rear gardens may also be appropriate here to avoid their being excessively shaded. Other factors will inevitably come into play, such as views and access to open space, the adverse impact of a very busy road or pavement on the edge of the development, sloping sites, existing trees to be retained or the potential for new tree planting. It is important to analyse, weigh and balance all these issues before arriving at a fully considered design resolution.

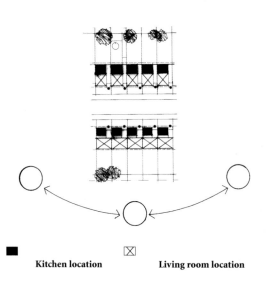

■ **Kitchen location**   ☒ **Living room location**

Solar orientation is an important consideration in the location of the principal habitable rooms. In this example, dwellings on different sides of the street have their living rooms arranged for optimum solar orientation

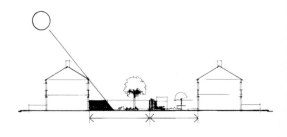

Lengthening rear gardens to take account of solar orientation can ensure that each garden receives an equal amount of sunlight

Flexibility, adaptability and change

Many homes are still sold in terms of the number of bedrooms, reception rooms and bathrooms, but modern construction methods (including the prefabrication of wide-span floors) can provide larger, multi-purpose spaces or space which residents can then subdivide to meet their own particular requirements.

Open plan and cellular forms imply different trade-offs and lifestyle choices. These include:

Open Plan	Cellular
May reduce market acceptability	Market norm
Flexible	Fixed
Spatially efficient	Spatially inefficient
Acoustic problems	Acoustic separation
Improves daylight penetration	Reduces daylight penetration

The use of partition doors between habitable rooms can provide some of the benefits of a large flexible space combined with the ability to form two smaller and separate rooms. Closing down a room can, for example, form a temporary guest bedroom or a quiet area for home-working or open it up to create a more generous space for entertaining or children's play. Careful planning of circulation spaces such as landing areas can also ensure that they perform more than their strictly utilitarian function of providing access to habitable rooms, and become multi-use spaces in their own right.

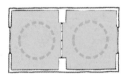

Space broken into small cells to separate out uses

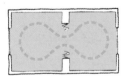

Merged space joins uses together

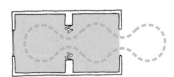

Borrowed garden space provides an extension to a habitable room

Adaptability

History suggests that the demand for different types of housing and for different uses in an area will evolve over time, both in response to changing socio-economic circumstances and to changing perceptions of an area. Both the Jesmond, Newcastle and the Stanstead Road, Lewisham case study areas have taken on a richer mix of housing types over time through the conversion of some dwellings to apartments, while Canning Street, Liverpool has seen some of its dwellings converted first to apartments, then to commercial use and finally back to single family houses.

Certain historic housing forms have proved very adaptable to changing requirements. Here, large town houses built for wealthy merchants have been converted to apartments and offices. Canning Street, Liverpool

The important design principle which flows from this is that dwellings and residential neighbourhoods which are designed to be adaptable will prove more robust over time than those which have been tailored tightly to a particular need. For example:

- steel and concrete frame construction can create broader spans which make the reconfiguration of internal space easier than where dwellings are built in a cellular form with loadbearing walls;
- vertical stacking of kitchens and bathrooms can simplify the provision of additional services;
- compact vertical circulation with ready means of escape can make larger houses more suitable for sub-division into apartments or commercial use;
- the use of solid floors can reduce noise transmission.

These considerations may be particularly relevant in town centre and edge-of-centre locations where the demand for different uses is likely to change over time.

Meeting the changing needs of residents

The needs of a household will evolve as a result of changing circumstances as well as a consequence of evolving social and workplace trends. These changes may result in the need for more, less or different domestic space, or in using the available space for different purposes.

'Lifetime homes' are designed to be adaptable to residents changing requirements and, particularly, in terms of providing for reduced personal mobility[3]. Taking the implications of reduced mobility into account in the initial design of the dwelling can ensure that the home can be adapted, for example, to provide:

- a stair lift;
- a room downstairs which could be used as a bedroom;
- access to a downstairs toilet which can be adapted to include a shower.

'Smart' technology is increasingly being used within the home, especially to provide support to older, less mobile people. For example, to foster contact with wardens and carers, to detect falls or lack of movement within the home or simply to cut off the water before a bath overflows. Once again, the installation of such technology in existing homes can be made easier and cheaper if it is provided for in the initial design. Skirting ducts, for example, which are easily accessible, can allow new cabling to be installed with minimal disruption.

Green issues   Energy issues   Flexibiltiy   Lifetime homes

Sustainability ⟷ Dwelling design

Smart technology

Delivering services   Communications   Monitoring

Smart technology can play an important role in supporting residents and reducing resource consumption

The option of creating additional living space or of making existing space meet needs better can enable a household to adapt to changing circumstances without its occupants having to move home by:

- extending the dwelling to the rear or side (but also possibly upwards);
- converting loft space into living space;
- reconfiguring existing space to form differently sized rooms.

Initial design and choices of construction method can have an important bearing on this potential. At a broader level, the provision of a wide range of housing opportunities across a neighbourhood can enable people to move to more suitable housing while maintaining family and friendship ties or retaining continuity in children's education or childcare.

Using loft spaces can be an effective way of meeting the need for more living space within the home. The potential for loft conversion can be as enhanced by careful attention to roof truss design as well the potential to modify the internal layout to satisfy fire regulations

Designing to maximise flexibility and choice in the use of internal and external space

The floor plans illustrated below show the potential for housing to be designed which is adaptable to changing occupier requirements. This particular housing was designed as part of an experimental scheme for Birmingham City Council by Shillam+Smith Architecture, and Urbanism.

The design approach emerged from a programme of consultation with the local community, a large proportion of which is of South Asian origin. This identified the first priorities for new homes as being affordability and space. To accommodate this, the houses were designed to be 20% larger than comparable new housing, but built for the same price, which meant a simple, no-frills layout. However, the houses were designed to be extendable so that residents could stamp their own identity on their homes.

The structure selected was a concrete frame, and extensions were intended to be within the capability of a local builder or a DIY enthusiast. In this way, housing could be provided which could accommodate the diversity of family types we find today. For example, people could decide whether they wanted a single living room or two, and exactly how they wanted bedroom arrangements. As families grow, and as residents become more affluent, the house could be extended to meet changing needs.

The basic shell, although simple, was robust, and satisfied the needs of building regulations and lifetime homes. Houses were also designed so that people can carry out a business from the 'front room' or even convert it into a shop.

Circulation
Kitchens & bathrooms
Bedrooms
Living rooms & dinning rooms
Balcony or terrace

Second floor

First floor

Ground floor

| Basic unit | 4 bedrooms open-plan living | 4 bedrooms 2 living rooms | Large ground floor extension | Ground floor office | Ground floor office |

Design thinking, building technology and residents' aspirations are continually evolving. Murray Grove, Hackney

Innovation

Current practice can prove restrictive in terms of flexibility in space planning, both internally and externally.

However, there is an emerging body of new practice and some local authorities are proving far more open to change and innovation than others. It is important to remain in touch with the 'leading edge' exemplars of practice and regulation. The potential for re-thinking of terrace and deep-plan housing and apartment design, of light wells, roof gardens and balconies, overlooking distances and rear garden lengths and quality communal gardens through imaginative design should be encouraged rather than falling on the tried, tested and readily permissible. This process can go hand in hand with initiatives optimising solar gain, energy efficiency and 'life time homes'.

Some key points

In thinking about space within and around the home, the following key aspects needs to be considered:

Internal / External Relationships

- Has an analysis been made of the relationships between internal and external space and has this informed the development of the scheme?

Places and Spaces

- Have external spaces – to the front and rear of dwellings, and those common to more than one dwelling – been thoroughly planned as quality spaces and as an integral part of the development?

Adaptability

- Do the layout and design of dwellings allow for future adaptation to meet changing needs?
- Have dwellings been designed so as to provide viable opportunities for future extension?

End notes:
1 See, for example, Part C of Standards and Quality in Development: a Good Practice Guide (National Housing Federation 1998) and Chapters 5-9 of the Housing Quality Indicators (DETR and the Housing Corporation 2000).
2 See, for example, Standards and Quality in Development: A Good Practice Guide, (National Housing Federation 1998).
3 Designing Lifetime Homes (Joseph Rowntree Foundation 1997) provides a detailed explanation of the concept of lifetime homes and provides guidance on appropriate design standards.

07

Thoroughness in design

- The importance of thoroughness
- Building elements
- Interface elements
- Landscape
- Consistency and continuing involvement
- Some key points

'In determining planning applications, local planning authorities should reject poor design . . . applicants for planning permission for housing development should be able to demonstrate how they have taken account of the need for good layout and design and how their proposals reflect the guidance set out in this PPG.'

PPG3: Housing paragraph 63

The importance of thoroughness

The richness and sense of quality seen in the best environments are the consequence of careful consideration of the detailed design of the buildings and the spaces and interfaces between them. This is the focus of this Chapter. It is concerned with the architecture, the 'streetscape' - the hard and soft landscape - and the threshold between private and public space. These are the concerns which will ultimately distinguish the quality of place created. However well planned and structured, a disappointing scheme is likely to result if it is not well executed at the level of detail.

This Chapter cannot and does not purport to be a detailed design manual. There is a great deal of relevant material elsewhere on the many aspects involved. The key messages of this Chapter are firstly, that detailed design is a key element in the creation of places of enduring quality and secondly, that regardless of the design guidance provided, high quality design, especially in relation to matters of detail, needs highly skilled designers.

It needs to be emphasised that there is no single appropriate design response. Quality comes in many forms. Indeed, in order to be responsive and fitting to different contexts, it is important to recognise the validity of a diverse range of approaches.

The lesson which is most clearly conveyed by the case studies is the fundamental importance of a coherent and integrated approach to the detailed design of a place.

In a quality place, the components from which it is made are fully resolved. This requires a fusion of all elements; the building, landscape and the interface between them. All components need to have been designed and constructed with the overall scheme, its character and quality, in mind. The best schemes do not appear to comprise buildings, a road and the bits in between, but rather form a place where the elements belong seamlessly to each other.

This is all too often not the case. The architect plans the buildings and general layout; the engineer designs the roads and services and negotiates with the authorities involved; the landscape architect then deals with the spaces in between. On occasion, certain of these design professions are not involved at all. A sense of completeness and cohesion is unlikely to emerge from such an approach, especially where the key visual elements at the interfaces (fences, walls and so on) are 'retro-fitted'. The road, in particular, has to be designed as an element of the urban landscape as well as being fit for purpose. Equally, the landscape design needs to complement the buildings and vice versa.

All details handled in a thoroughgoing way to create a quality place. Upper Brook Hill, Woodstock

Building elements

The quality of the building can be spoilt by poor attention to detail. The individual elements of which buildings of any kind are composed have a key role in determining their quality. To contribute successfully to the whole they need to be well designed in their own right, and arranged in a coherent and legible way which is consistent with the overall architectural approach. The parts contribute to a whole which has integrity. This is nothing to do with architectural styles, or, necessarily, with tradition. The best domestic architecture of all ages has abounded with invention and even fun.

It is at the level of the individual elements that the viewer makes the connection with the human scale, an important part of achieving places of quality. When the elements are brought together in a coherent way, whether with deliberate uniformity or deliberate variety, they build up to a larger scale - the house, the block, the street - which in turn is comprehensible. For example, the terraced housing at Greenland Passage, Southwark provides a useful illustration of the skillful arrangement of the elements of a facade which makes use of modelling and shadow and sets up a rhythm. The strength of the detailed design is such that it can successfully accommodate garage doors.

Splendid articulation and rhythm of gables, bays, balconies and the facade create a human scale despite the large bulk of the building. Elgin Avenue, Maida Vale

The same success as illustrated above can also be achieved with contemporary forms and materials. Century Court, Cheltenham

Building elements

The building elements which require careful attention in detailed design include:
- doors
- windows
- porches
- roof structures
- lighting
- flues and ventilation
- gutters, pipes and other rainwater details
- balconies
- garage doors
- ironmongery and decorative features
- flashings

It is vital not only to view these elements in isolation, but also to consider how they come together to form the whole and to examine carefully the 'joins' between the elements.

Strong design treatment of windows and balconies draws attention away from potentially intrusive garage doors which are also skilfully handled. Greenland Passage, Southwark

A good corner. The ground floor internal planning of schemes of this type is very important to create an acceptable internal living space. Narrow Street, Tower Hamlets

There is also a danger of seeing the detailed design response as either 'traditional' or 'modern'. Such debates about style can get in the way of producing a distinctive quality response to the design challenges involved. Traditional materials and design ideas can be used in a totally modern way. Conversely, new materials and cutting-edge construction technologies can be deployed to create a comfortable human scale architecture and, where appropriate, reflect traditional styles.

Whatever the language and idioms of the architecture, there is a need to understand their structure and logic as well as appearance. These issues affect design subtly and at different scales. In any design or idiom, the approach needs to involve an iterative process between the massing and form of the building and its detailed components. As with everything else in this guide, there is no substitute for design skill.

The scale of the terrace is articulated at roof height by the elegantly glazed dormers and the occasional change in plan and height. Jesmond, Newcastle

A well articulated roofline, a strong horizontal parapet and well proportioned fenestration all contribute to the quality of this scheme. Even the guttering and vents are used to punctuate the facade and contribute to the sense of proportion. Brightlingsea Place, Tower Hamlets

Modelling, colour, shadow and clear detailing throughout. Note the frosted glass for privacy in the lower level windows and the discrete venting of the undercroft parking. However, the steps would not meet current requirements for level access. Ocean Wharf, Tower Hamlets

The elevational components are carefully designed to relate to the overall form and mass of the scheme. Coptic Street, Camden

Thoroughness in design

Interface elements

Doorways, thresholds, gardens and the enclosures to gardens need particular attention in order to appear a fitting and integral part of the overall scheme. The entrance and threshold of buildings are intensively used and many competing needs have to be co-ordinated in their layout and design. The design can be enhanced by:

- using a limited palette of materials;
- detailing the composition of railings and walls to create a permeable front boundary while screening or containing the elements;
- including a porch or stoop which can absorb storage space within its flank walls without compromising security concerns;
- organising storage arrangements so that views from public areas and from windows within the home are not interrupted;
- carefully detailed lighting which can provide an attractive sense of welcome as well as security.

The interface elements

The interface elements which require careful attention in detailed design include:

- bin storage
- cycle storage
- external lighting
- meter boxes
- service entries
- inspection boxes
- storage for recycling of waste
- cool storage for home deliveries
- windows and glazing
- walls, hedges, fences, and gates
- space for drying clothes

These elements need to be considered and designed as an integral part of the overall scheme. A simple test is that if the elements are hardly noticeable then the design is successful.

A simple, clear and composed threshold. Lighting, security, meters and planting all accommodated and the wall height is just at a level which hides the bin. Chillingworth Road, Islington

The interface at the rear of dwellings can also be important, especially where communal gardens, courts or rear access are involved. As the Friars Quay, Norwich case study shows, the traditional two metre high rear wall can provide good quality security and privacy to ground floor rooms and garden/patio areas. The communal or public faces of walls and fences benefit from well defined and maintained planting. Low or close boarded fences are difficult to handle in these respects.

The potential impact of courtyard parking on the privacy and quality of rear garden space requires very careful consideration, Poundbury, Dorchester illustrates an ingenious response where some of the dwellings face the courtyards (see page 57).

A traditional brick wall provides good privacy and security to rear gardens. Friars Quay, Norwich

Without careful design rear courtyard parking can undermine the privacy and quality of rear gardens as well as reducing the space available for gardens

'Landscaping should be an integral part of new development and opportunities should be taken for the retention of existing trees and shrubs, and for new plantings.'

PPG3: Housing paragraph 52

Landscape

Landform, natural features and their ecology are always important. Trees, shrubs, flowers and grass and their containment require particular attention. The retention and use of existing trees and, on occasion, walls, ramps, steps and hedges can give a sense of maturity and distinction. New planting needs careful and specialised consideration according to locale and practicality. Soils, drainage, sunlight and shelter are critical factors as well as the use, where possible, of native species.

Where close to buildings, a strong maintenance regime is essential for hedges, shrubs and grass. All planting elements need well defined edges which can be formed by properly designed walls, kerbs, tree grilles and the like. Using the positioning of the buildings, rather than the road and statutory setbacks, or sight lines remains the most effective way of defining the space. The principle of 'tracking' is useful here (see Chapter 3[1]).

Well planted front gardens perfectly suited to the scale of the buildings. Isledon Village, Islington

Landscape elements

The landscape elements which require careful consideration in detailed design include:
- trees, flowers, grass and other planting
- the carriageways, footways and floorscape
- cycle–ways
- kerbs
- steps and ramps
- fences, walls, hedges and gates
- inspection boxes and covers
- tree grilles
- street signage
- street lighting
- seats
- bollards
- railings
- public art
- wayleaves and easements

The detailed alignment of carriageways, footpaths and any front garden or threshold space before the building edge involves the consideration of many elements including: pedestrian, cycle and vehicle needs; on-street parking and service requirements; underground services; and landscape features.

The street needs to be considered as an important element of detailed design. A well-designed space will accommodate street furniture, signage and other elements in a calm, unemphatic way. In general, this is often a case of 'less' being 'more'.

It is always important to avoid clutter. Buildings, walls and fences can in some circumstances be used to mount road signs and lighting upon, but attention to the need for wayleaves and easements to allow for their installation and maintenance will be important. Cables should be undergrounded as far as possible. Inspection boxes should be recessed in the planting and street furniture should not clutter pavements.

The design of sitting-out areas provides a framework for planting in an intimate courtyard. Webster Yard, Kendal

Shrubs and trees screen parking areas and soften the 'join' between the buildings and the street. Bedford Court, Doncaster

No signs, no bollards, no road markings and simple lighting. A clutter-free environment. Friars Quay, Norwich

Retro-fitting of bollards and signs rather spoil a well planned local space. Isledon Village, Islington

The floorscape is particularly important. Traffic calming measures need to be designed in as an integral part of the layout and draw from a well chosen palette of materials. There are places where shared surfaces will be appropriate and vehicles can be slowed by such devices as narrow carriageways and surfaces of setts, paviors and slabs. Again, less can be more.

Good quality lighting can make an important contribution to the attractiveness of an area, in terms of the quality of its appearance during both daylight hours and night time, as well as to its safety and public security. There is increasing emphasis on lighting for walking, cycling and amenity as well as driving and upon the reduction of light pollution. It is important that lighting engineers are involved at an early stage in the project design. The design of the columns and luminaires in obviously critical. There are other possibilities – wall mounting, bollards with integral lights, and ground level up-lighters which are appropriate in some circumstances.

Consistency and continuing commitment

Creating high quality residential environments requires a continuing commitment to quality and detailed design right through to the completion and handover of the scheme. There are a number of areas where attention is important:

- avoiding 'retro-fittings' and 'bolt-ons';
- consulting early with statutory, regulatory and adoption agencies and specialist advisers on such matters as lighting, security and road safety;
- determining the nature of future maintenance, adoption and service regimes and responsibilities. This is particularly important for landscape planning and design.

Attention to these matters can help both to avoid obvious or glaring mistakes and to create a sense of quality through the harmony of all the components. Indeed, ingenious detailed solutions in resolving such matters can enrich a scheme.

Rigorous attention to detail and the integration of landscape and building elements. Century Court, Cheltenham

Children's play dictated the need for a gate to this family housing scheme. The gate is celebrated as public art and lifts the whole scheme. Dragon Court, Camden

The quality of the public realm can be undermined through:

- the lack of a full landscape plan and specification as part of the design of the scheme submitted for planning approval;
- inadequate and unrealistic budgets for external works, particularly for hard and soft landscape;
- a tendency for the budgets for these items to be reduced in an attempt to cover over-runs in work undertaken earlier in the construction process;
- the problems of accommodating late additions, especially those required by the adoption agencies.

These issues apply to all forms of housing development, but it is important to appreciate that as the density of development rises and/or the intensity of use increases, so too does the importance of a complete and robust landscape treatment.

The overriding objective has to be to generate a culture where there is a commitment to the creation of enduring value through investment in the landscape and associated works rather than cost minimisation. The selection of materials for the external works always needs to be subject to the same rigour as has been applied to the buildings themselves.

Here the relationship with the street is maintained with car parking in a semi-basement, set back from the footpath and the boundary wall. Holland Park, Kensington

Timber fence on indeterminate alignment and without a planting edge lets down this scheme

Integral garages can create a lifeless, dead frontage effect while at the same time not accommodating many cars. Here quality is further eroded by the mismatch between the raised surface and the length of cars on the forecourt as well as by oil stains and painted road markings

Some key points

In appraising the detailed design of any new development, the following key points should be considered:

Completeness

- Does the scheme feel complete, integrated and cohesive in architectural, engineering and landscape terms?
- Have each of the building, interface and landscape elements been considered in detailed design terms?
- Are all the difficult and potentially intrusive elements in the elevations, the doorways and thresholds and in the street dealt with in a manner which will make them almost unnoticeable?

Application of design skills

- Has the design team included the full range of skills (in architecture, urban design, engineering, landscape architecture and other specialisms appropriate to the characteristics of the site) needed to create a quality residential environment?
- Have these skills been deployed in an integrated way throughout the design process?

Thinking ahead

- Is there evidence in the detailed design of consultation and advance planning with the service agencies, the planning, building and adoption authorities?
- Is there a full landscape plan, detailed specification and budget? Is there real commitment to its implementation as an integral part of the development?

Distinctiveness

- Is the scheme tailored to reflect its circumstances and surroundings or is it the application of standard housing types and layout forms?
- Has there been an effort in the architecture and space planning to create a distinctive and quality place? Are the corners dealt with authoritatively? Is there any left-over space?

End notes:

1 Places Streets and Movement: a companion guide to Design Bulletin 32 (DETR 1998) is a key reference for the design of movement routes in residential areas.

Appendix

About the case studies

This Appendix presents background information on the 12 case study areas which have been examined in the course of preparing the guide. These areas were selected to examine how the attributes of successful housing, as identified from a literature and practice review (see page 12), have been applied in relation to different forms of housing in different contexts around the country.

The case studies include well known developments, some of which have won awards for their design, but they also include more humble examples of 'ordinary' housing which can be found in towns and cities across the country. The case studies are not therefore intended to represent the very best examples of particular aspects of design; rather they are presented as places which work well in the round when viewed against a range of urban design principles.

It must be stressed however, that the case studies are not presented as templates which can simply be copied. Rather, as with the guide itself, they are intended to stimulate thinking about better practice in the layout and design of new housing including learning lessons from their weaknesses as well as their strengths.

The case studies include a broad range of housing forms and densities; from suburban houses developed as urban extensions through to high density city-centre apartments. There is, however, a conscious bias towards housing in the density range of 30 to 50 dwellings to the hectare. This reflects the fact that one of the principal challenges facing local authorities and developers is how to improve the quality and increase the density of housing, which in recent years has been built at average densities of 20 to 25 dwellings to the hectare and below.

The information presented for each of the case studies includes a general evaluation of the strengths and weaknesses of the area and more detailed comparable data on, for example, density, levels of car parking provision, dwelling sizes and housing mix. In some cases this data relates to a smaller sub-area within the overall case study area.

The case studies are presented in ascending order of density. However, it should be remembered that the historic case studies can be viewed both in terms of the densities at which they were originally built and at the densities which exist today following, for example, the subdivision of houses into flats. For consistency these historic areas are presented in terms of their original density, but with an estimate of the current post-conversion density. The information on car parking provision and other matters is in respect of the original form of development unless indicated otherwise.

The case studies

	Thorley Lane, Bishops Stortford	**30 – 50** dwellings per hectare
	Stanstead Road, Lewisham, London	
	Poundbury, Dorchester	
	Canning Street, Liverpool	
	Highsett, Cambridge	
	Jesmond, Newcastle	
	Friars Quay, Norwich	**50 – 100** dwellings per hectare
	Rolls Crescent, Hulme, Manchester	
	Greenland Passage, Southwark, London	
	Isledon Village, Islington, London	
	Deansgate Quay, Manchester	**100 +** dwellings per hectare
	Webster's Yard, Kendal	

Thorley Lane, Bishops Stortford

Built
1997

Lead designer
Melville Dunbar Associates

Developer
Countryside Properties

Local authority
East Hertfordshire District Council

Overview

Thorley Lane is located on the periphery of Bishops Stortford, an historic market town in Hertfordshire. The scheme forms part of the much larger St Michael's Mead Development. The site is accessed through earlier suburban detached and semi- detached housing arranged in a pattern of culs-de-sac which seems to have been dictated largely by highway standards. Thorley Lane shows how a place of distinct quality can be created on the urban edge.

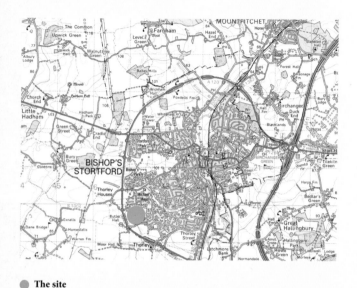

● The site

Area of detailed analysis ● Photo position

0   50m

Evaluation

Thorley Lane includes a number of positive features:
- The development creates an urban environment that displays many of the Essex Design Guide principles, but the architectural style is sometimes inconsistent with an eclectic use of traditional building materials;
- Houses have been set forward to the street to form a continuous built frontage. A two metre buffer between the street and the building line also provides a degree of privacy for residents;

- There is a high level of natural surveillance and a sense of place;
- Pinch point gateways and curves to the street limit visual monotony and create varied spatial experiences along the route, particularly for the pedestrian.

However a less satisfactory aspect of the development is that parking takes up a high proportion of the site.

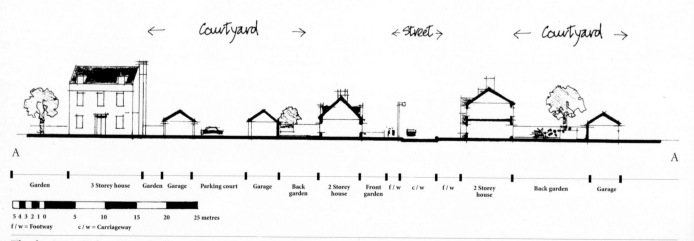

← Courtyard →   ← Street →   ← Courtyard →

A   A

Garden | 3 Storey house | Garden | Garage | Parking court | Garage | Back garden | 2 Storey house | Front garden | f/w | c/w | f/w | 2 Storey house | Back garden | Garage

5 4 3 2 1 0   5   10   15   20   25 metres

f / w = Footway   c / w = Carriageway

① The natural curve in the street slows cars, reduces visual monotony and provides a varied spatial experience, particularly for the pedestrian.

② Houses have been set forward to the street to form a continuous built frontage offering a high level of natural surveillance and sense of place.

③ Because of its location, the development is unashamedly tailored to commuting. Parking courts are accessed through openings in the street frontage.

④ The architectural style is often eclectic.

⑤ The potential of building corners and entries has not always been fully exploited.

Analysis of built form components within the area of detailed analysis	
Area of detailed analysis:	0.9 ha.
Number of dwellings:	28
Dwelling mix: (16 house types)	2+3+5-bed terraced 2+3+4-bed detached 3+4-bed semi-detached
Density	
Dwellings per hectare:	31
Habitable rooms per hectare:	133
Floorspace per hectare:	5440m²
Space in and around the home	
3-bed house:	108 m²
Typical garden area for a 3-bed house:	114 m²
5-bed house:	234 m²
Typical garden area [for a 5-bed house]:	149 m²
Car parking	
Parking spaces per dwelling:	1.9
Parking within building curtilage:	0
On-street:	0%
Parking courts/ dedicated off-street bays/shelters:	49%
Garages:	51%
Overall land budget	
Dwellings footprint:	26%
Private gardens:	38%
Communal outdoor space and courtyards:	0%
Roads, footpaths and parking:	36%

Thorley Lane, Bishops Stortford

Stanstead Road, Lewisham

Built
1885-1914

Lead designer/developer
Developed by speculative
builders on 99-year leases

Local authority
The Local Authority was Lewisham
Local Board. The relevant building
controls were the London Building
Acts, supervised by a District
Surveyor

Overview

The Stanstead Road area is located between Catford and Forest Hill in south-east London. The area was developed between 1885-1914 to meet the growing demand for suburban middle-class housing and to exploit the opportunities provided by the developing railway and tram networks. Within our area of detailed analysis, two main house styles were originally built: firstly, five-bedroom semi-detached houses, followed by a later development of three-bedroom terraced houses on the classic bye-law pattern. A number of dwellings of each type have since been sub-divided into flats for sale or rent, reflecting a strong demand for smaller homes close to good suburban rail connections to Central London.

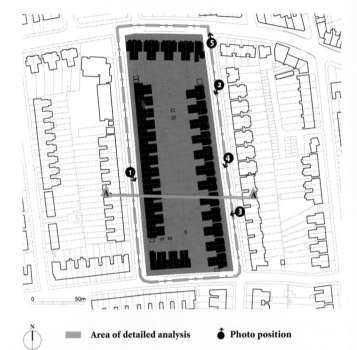

● The site   N   0   50m   ▬ Area of detailed analysis   ⚲ Photo position

Evaluation

There are many positive features of this area. These include:
- The format of the street block which creates a highly permeable form and allows for on-street parking;
- The original sizes of dwellings are robust for future adaptability;
- Adequate garden size allows for a variety of different uses and the boundary treatments create a high level of privacy;
- Building frontage and garden walling provides complete enclosure of private rear gardens.

Conversely, over time a large number of front gardens have been converted into off-street parking spaces, which has undermined the quality of the street scene. There is also a high level of street and front garden clutter due to the lack of screening for bins. In common with Victorian housing the treatment of corners has resulted in areas of dead frontage, some of which have suffered from graffiti.

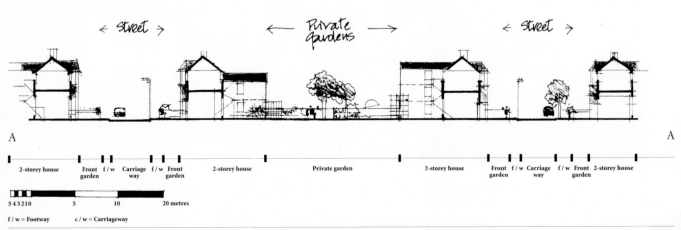

| 2-storey house | Front garden | f / w | Carriage way | f / w | Front garden | 2-storey house | Private garden | 2-storey house | Front garden | f / w | Carriage way | f / w | Front garden | 2-storey house |

5 4 3 2 1 0   5   10   20 metres

f / w = Footway   c / w = Carriageway

❶ The perimeter street layout yields a robust and permeable form.

❷ Large, semi-detached houses form spacious family homes or two/three smaller apartments.

❸ Good sized gardens provide for a variety of uses.

❹ Building frontage and garden gates completely enclose of rear gardens.

❺ Stanstead Road contains a mix of uses, such as the Post Office; that supports the local community.

Analysis of built form components within the area of detailed analysis	
Area of detailed analysis:	2.1 ha.
Number of dwellings:	66 dwellings (98 dwellings including conversions)
Dwelling mix (2 house types):	5 – bed semi-detached 3 – bed terraced houses
Density (as originally built)	
Dwellings per hectare:	31
Habitable rooms per hectare:	220
Floor space per hectare:	5483m^2
Space in and around the home	
5-bed semi-detached house:	204 m^2
Typical garden area:	172 m^2
3-bed terraced house:	171 m^2
Typical garden area:	130 m^2
Car parking (not including front garden parking)	
Parking spaces per dwelling:	1.2
Parking within the curtilage of building:	0%
On-street:	100%
Communal outdoor space and courtyards:	0%
Garages:	0%
Overall land budget	
Dwellings footprint:	26%
Private gardens:	55%
Parking courts/ dedicated off-street bays:	0%
Roads, footpaths and parking:	19%

Poundbury, Dorchester

Built	Developer
1993 onwards	Duchy of Cornwall
	CG Fry & Son
Lead designer	Morrish Builders, Guinness Trust
Leon Krier	
Alan Baxter and Associates	**Local authority**
	West Dorset District Council

Overview

Poundbury forms a planned urban extension on the western edge of Dorchester. The 168 hectare site adjoins existing housing on the east and agricultural land to the south and west; a bypass lies to the north. Phase One is 7.5 hectares in size; our area of detailed analysis within this phase is one hectare and is mainly composed of three and four bedroom terraced and detached houses.

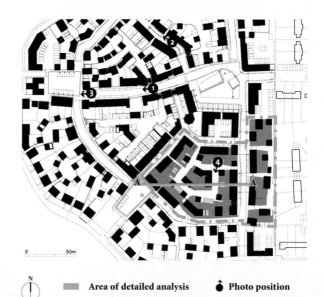

● The site

N ▬ Area of detailed analysis ♦ Photo position

0 50m

Evaluation

The scheme demonstrates the successful application of a number of urban design principles:

- Continuous street facades, largely uninterrupted by parking bays or garages. Cars are parked within internal courtyards, on-street or in bays located in residents' back gardens. This reinforces the distinction between public and private space with building facades built along the back-of-pavement line;
- Street lighting and signage, and, more importantly, road geometry, demonstrate a creative response to local authority standards. There is very little segregation of pedestrians and vehicles, but vehicle speeds are kept low by the careful alignment of streets.

- Social housing is well integrated with private housing in terms of both location and external appearance;
- Traditional materials have been used consistently throughout the scheme;
- There are impressive levels of maintenance and visual surveillance of the private and public realms. The former is achieved by covenants imposed on homeowners and the latter by on-site management control. There is little evidence of vandalism or crime.

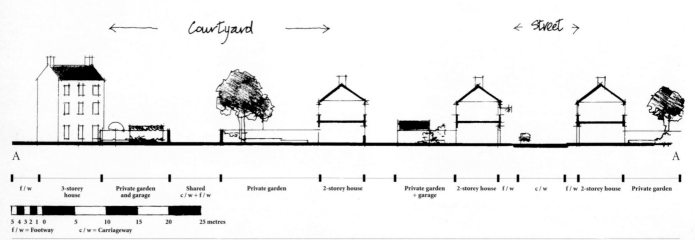

← Courtyard →   ← Street →

A   A

| f/w | 3-storey house | Private garden and garage | Shared c/w + f/w | Private garden | 2-storey house | Private garden + garage | 2-storey house | f/w | c/w | f/w | 2-storey house | Private garden |

5 4 3 2 1 0   5   10   15   20   25 metres
f/w = Footway   c/w = Carriageway

① Continuous street facades, unbroken by parking or garages.

② Street lighting, signage and road geometry, show a creative response to local authority standards.

③ Social housing is well integrated with private housing in terms both of its location and its external appearance.

④ There are high levels of maintenance and natural surveillance of all properties.

⑤ While the amount of parking at Poundbury, Dorchester is high, its arrangement provides residents with the choice of in-curtilage parking or larger back gardens.

Analysis of built form components within the area of detailed analysis	
Area of detailed analysis:	1 ha
Number of dwellings:	34
Dwelling mix (21 house types):	3 + 4 bed detached 2, 3 + 4 bed terraced Office + 3 bed flat
Density	
Dwellings per hectare:	34
Habitable rooms per hectare:	170
Floorspace per hectare:	7186m²
Space in and around the home	
3-bed house:	94m²
Typical garden area:	43m²
4-bed house:	116m²
Garden area:	54m²
Car parking	
Parking spaces per dwelling:	2.5
Parking within building curtilage:	35%
On street:	17%
Courts /dedicated off-street bays:	9%
Garages:	39%
Overall land budget	
Dwellings footprint:	25%
Private gardens:	34%
Communal outdoor space and courtyards:	0%
Roads, footpaths and parking:	41%

Poundbury, Dorchester

Canning Street, Liverpool

Built	**Local authority**
1835-1845	City of Liverpool
Lead designer / developer	
Speculative builders, on 75-year leases	

Overview

The Canning Street area is located close to the centre Liverpool and is in close proximity to the University and the Anglican Cathedral. The latter creates an impressive backdrop which is visible from many streets in the area.

The area was developed between 1835 and 1845 to provide some of the first housing beyond the city centre. The dwellings in the Canning Street area were originally designed as three to four storey five-bedroom family houses.

Many of these dwellings have been sub-divided into flats, some housing students. The only regulations in force at the time of construction were over sewerage and paving. Part of our area of detailed analysis also includes Egerton Street, which is a street of two-storey three-bed terraced houses. The majority of these dwellings are still three-bed houses.

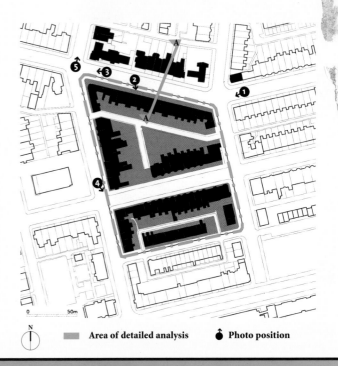

● The site

● N   ▪ Area of detailed analysis   ● Photo position

Evaluation

Successful qualities of the area of analysis are:
*   The scale of the street combined with the building heights engender a feeling of openness and space, despite the relatively high densities. Pavements are generously sized for the pedestrian and street lighting is good;
*   A continuous building frontage provides surveillance of the street as well as encouraging street activity. There is also a clear separation between the public street and the private dwelling through the combination of a continuous frontage and a short enclosed buffer of planting;

However some of the end-of-terrace blind flanks of buildings have attracted grafitti as well as abandoned refuse.

The back alleys are also a point of concern. Although well-maintained and well-lit, providing a suitable location for bin collection and servicing, they also create concerns on safety and security issues.

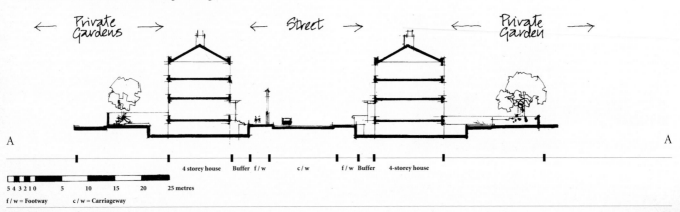

1 Street widths are overly generous and only just balanced by the height of the buildings. Wide pavements help to create a sense of safety for the pedestrian.

2 Continuous frontage provides for good street surveillance as well as for on-street activity.

3 Views of Liverpool's Anglican Cathedral enhance the area.

4 Blank facades attract vandalism as well as abandoned litter.

5 Active frontages are formed by 'wrapping' a building around a street corner.

Analysis of built form components within the area of detailed analysis	
Area of detailed analysis:	1.9 ha
Number of dwellings:	78 original now 250 dwellings through subdivision
Dwelling mix (Two original house types):	5 – bed town houses 3 – bed houses
Density	
Dwellings per hectare:	Originally 41 dwellings/ hectare (current density 119 dwellings/ hectare)
Original habitable rooms per hectare:	341
Floorspace per hectare:	9919 m²
Space in and around the home	
5-bed townhouse:	204 m²
Typical garden area:	81 m²
3-bed terrace house	92 m²
Typical garden area:	19 m²
Car Parking	
Parking spaces per dwelling:	1.5
Parking within building curtilage:	0%
On-street:	85%
Parking courts/ dedicated off-street bays/shelters:	3%
Garages:	12%
Overall land budget	
Dwellings footprint:	37%
Private gardens:	35%
Communal outdoor space and courtyards:	0%
Roads, footpaths and parking:	28%

Canning Street, Liverpool

Highsett, Cambridge

Built 1959-1964	**Local authority** Cambridge City Council
Lead designer Eric Lyons & Partners	
Developer Wates, Rattee & Kett	

Overview

Highsett was developed between 1959-1964. Its 4 hectare site is divided into three distinct types of housing: Phase one: The Quad (flats and large communal garden); Phase two: The 'L' shaped (2-storey houses) and Phase three (our case study area): a cul-de-sac of townhouses. The development benefits greatly from its location just outside the centre of Cambridge and from the existing mature landscape.

Highsett is built in a gault brick, typical of East Anglia; roofs are pitched inwards to a central gutter and roof glazing is used to light bathrooms and staircases. By present-day standards, rather large areas of glazing are used. The houses are arranged in short terraces with small private walled gardens.

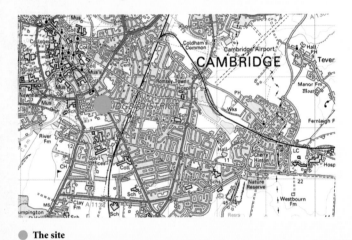

● The site

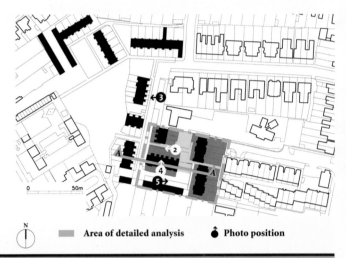

■ Area of detailed analysis ⬆ Photo position

Evaluation

Successful features of the area of detailed analysis are:
- Each house has a well-screened private garden or courtyard;
- There are safe, overlooked areas for children to play in;
- bin stores, bicycles and meter boxes can also be easily accommodated in these enclosed front gardens;
- A mix of short terraces fronting the street as well as those positioned in parallel, help to provide a high level of natural surveillance onto pathways and communal spaces, but not necessarily onto the street;
- Mature landscaped areas, albeit that some trees are very close to the buildings.

The area of detailed analysis demonstrates that a clear division of private and public space is important. However, one block appears to have been originally designed with a communal

back, but subsequently the space has been subdivided and used for private parking.

Other concerns are the poor design of the grouped garages as a long row with a large area of hardstanding in front. It is not clear whether these are viewed as satisfactory by residents, as some have converted their forecourts into parking spaces.

Although the site is structured as a cul-de-sac, it is quite permeable, due to its numerous pedestrian paths, but the configuration of the site and these multiple pathways, some enclosed by walls, and the proximity to an urban environment must create some security risks.

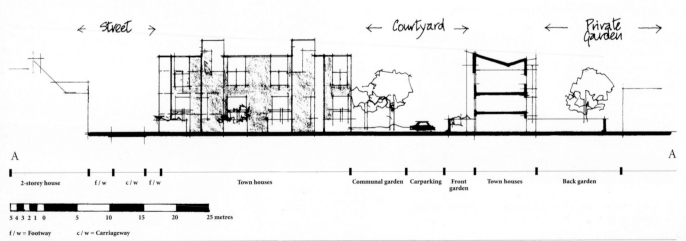

① The careful design of the front gardens provides space for bins, bicycles and meter boxes.

② There is a high level of surveillance onto pathways and communal spaces, but not necessarily onto the street. This must create some security risks.

③ The external architectural design of the houses is straightforward and does not suffer from the more negative features of their period.

④ One block appears to have been originally designed with a communal back, but the space has been subdivided and is used for private parking.

⑤ It is not clear whether the garages are viewed as satisfactory by residents, as some have converted forecourts into parking spaces.

Analysis of built form components in the area of detailed analysis	
Area of detailed analysis:	0.4 ha.
Number of Dwellings:	18
Dwelling mix:	2-storey terrace
2 house types	3-storey townhouse
Density	
Dwellings per hectare:	45
Habitable rooms per hectare:	203
Floorspace per hectare:	4953 m^2
Space in and around the home	
2-bed house: (2-storey)	88 m^2
Typical garden area:	23 m^2
4-bed house: (3-storey)	120 m^2
Typical garden area:	63 m^2
Car Parking	
Parking spaces per dwelling:	1.2
Parking within building curtilage:	17%
On-street:	5%
Parking courts/ dedicated off-street bays:	22%
Garages:	56%
Overall land budget	
Dwellings footprint:	24%
Private gardens:	43%
Communal outdoor space and courtyards:	7%
Roads, footpaths and parking:	26%

Highsett, Cambridge

Jesmond, Newcastle

Built 1870-1885	**Local authority** Newcastle City Council
Lead designer/developer Built by speculative builders	

Overview

Jesmond is a Victorian suburb to the north east of the centre of Newcastle. Our detailed area of analysis examines the two and three storey terraces between Queens Road and Grosvenor Road. The 4 hectare site originally contained 173 dwellings. Today, as the result of conversions of houses into flats, this total has risen to about 189 dwellings. Most houses in this area contain four bedrooms and often an average of seven habitable rooms per dwelling.

● The site

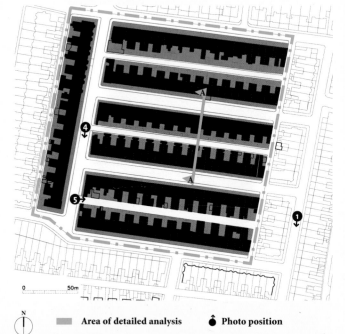

N | ▬ Area of detailed analysis | ▲ Photo position

Evaluation

There are many positive aspects of the area, including:
- The location of the area in terms of its strong public transport connections and the lower reliance on the car;
- On-street parking is along the terraces. The street also promotes a robust and permeable form, especially in terms of accessing surrounding shops and public transport facilities. Corner treatments have also been considered in the terrace design;
- There are no street trees, but the local scene is enhanced by extensive personalisation and landscaping;

- Adaptation of spaces has led to the use of back alleys for garages, extensions and courtyard gardens;

Outside the area of detailed analaysis large front gardens are often used as the primary play space. However, this raises security concerns and requires children's play to be closely supervised.

The back alleys are a point at issue. Although well-maintained, well-lit and providing a suitable location for bin storage and servicing, they also raise concerns over safety and security.

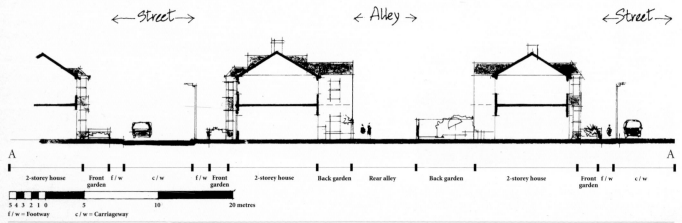

← Street →   ← Alley →   ← Street →

A ——— A

| 2-storey house | Front garden | f / w | c / w | f / w | Front garden | 2-storey house | Back garden | Rear alley | Back garden | 2-storey house | Front garden | f / w | c / w |

5 4 3 2 1 0   5   10   20 metres

f / w = Footway   c / w = Carriageway

① On-street parking slows down traffic and creates activity on the street.

② There are high levels of personalisation and landscaping.

③ Where large front gardens are sunny they are often used as a play space. However, this would require close supervision, given their proximity to the street

④ The perimeter block form provides direct and well over-looked pedestrian routes.

⑤ Back alleys provide an area to store rubbish and allow access into back spaces for car parking, but this raises concerns about safety and security.

Analysis of built form components within the area of detailed analysis	
Area of detailed analysis:	4 ha
Number of Dwellings (173 houses):	Originally 173 dwellings (Today 189 dwellings)
Dwelling mix (2 house types):	3 + bed terraced
Density (as originally built houses)	
Dwellings per hectare:	43
Habitable rooms per hectare:	253
Floorspace per hectare:	4846 m^2
Space in and around the home	
4-bed house:	297 m^2
Typical garden area for a 4-bed house:	58 m^2
Car parking	
Parking spaces per dwelling:	1.8
Parking within building curtilage:	0%
On-street:	89%
Parking courts/ dedicated off-street bays	0%
Garages	11%
Overall land budget	
Dwellings footprint:	41%
Private gardens:	26%
Communal outdoor space and courtyards:	0%
Roads, footpaths and parking:	33%

Jesmond, Newcastle

Friars Quay, Norwich

Built
1974

Local authority
City of Norwich

Lead designer
Fielden and Mawson Architects

Developer
City of Norwich and RG Carter Ltd

Overview

Friars Quay is located in the Colgate area at the centre of Norwich, bounded on one side by the River Wensum. Several historic churches surround the site, creating an attractive and varied streetscape. In the 1970s, a partnership between the

City of Norwich and local developer RG Carter Ltd was formed to redevelop this prominent city centre industrial site. The scheme of 40 four bedroom townhouses also included nine ground floor flats, intended for the elderly.

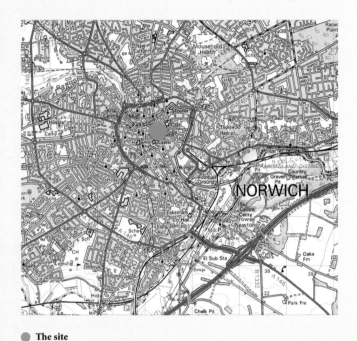

● The site

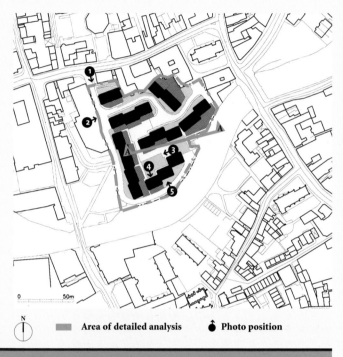

N

■ Area of detailed analysis   ● Photo position

0   50m

Evaluation

Friars Quay displays a number of strengths in its design:
- As a development, Friars Quay responds successfully to its city centre location;
- Although the scheme has a strong urban feel, this is softened through the diversity of planting and boundary treatments;
- Various parking techniques have been adopted, including on-plot parking when the curvature of the road permits it.
- The natural curve of the street also prevents visual monotony and slows car speeds down;

- Pedestrians have been given high priority and most communal areas are well overlooked and attractive pedestrian places.

The only negative aspect to highlight is the uncertain relationship of the fronts and backs of terraces to each other. This also results in rear gardens facing on to the public realm, although the gardens are well enclosed by brick walls.

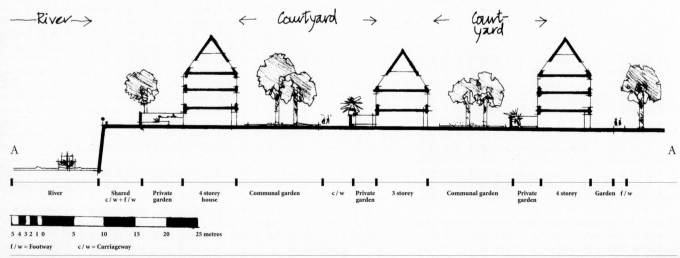

←River→   ←Courtyard→   ←Courtyard→

A   A

River | Shared c/w + f/w | Private garden | 4 storey house | Communal garden | c/w | Private garden | 3 storey | Communal garden | Private garden | 4 storey | Garden f/w

5 4 3 2 1 0   5   10   15   20   25 metres

f/w = Footway   c/w = Carriageway

❶ The scheme meshes with its surrounding context.

❷ The curve of the street prevents visual monotony, slows cars down and allows for on-plot parking.

❸ The scheme provides well overlooked pedestrian and communal areas. A mix of house types provides street surveillance at different times of the day.

❹ The building form represents an efficient use of space.

❺ The attractively varied roofscape is visible from street level.

Analysis of built form components within the area of detailed analysis	
Area of detailed analysis	0.9 ha
Number of Dwellings:	49 original dwellings (50 dwellings today)
Dwelling mix (3 dwelling types):	4-bed houses 1-bed flats 4-bed houses above ground floor flats.
Density (as originally built)	
Dwellings per hectare:	54
Habitable rooms per hectare:	183
Floorspace per hectare:	4392 m²
Space in and around the home	
4-bed house + integral garage:	177 m²
Typical garden area for a 4-bed house:	55 m²
1-bed flat:	52 m²
Typical garden area for a 1-bed flat:	none
Car Parking	
Parking spaces per dwelling:	1.5
Parking within building curtilage:	26%
On-street:	16%
Parking courts/ dedicated off-street bays/shelters:	28%
Garages:	30%
Overall land budget	
Dwellings footprint:	24%
Private gardens:	13%
Communal outdoor space and courtyards:	16%
Roads, footpaths and parking:	47%

Rolls Crescent, Hulme

Built 1997	**Local authority** Manchester City Council
Lead designer ECD Architects	
Developer North British Housing Association	

Overview

The site lies within the area developed as the infamous crescent blocks of the 1960s. Since 1991, under Hulme City Challenge, the area has undergone total regeneration. Rolls Crescent is a built response to the Hulme Design Guide and it could be said that this development provokes the sense of community and spirit expressed in the Guide.

The site follows a very traditional street layout and forms three distinctive perimeter blocks on the 1-hectare site. The development consists of a varied mix of house types on one, two and three storeys. Four of the 67 houses have been designed specifically for wheelchair access. Ramps have also been positioned outside a further four three-bedroom dwellings, intended for the elderly.

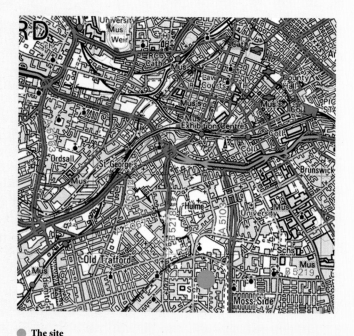

● The site

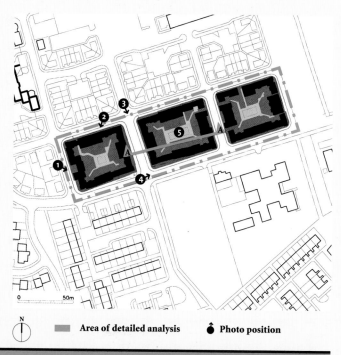

0   50m

N

▬ Area of detailed analysis   ● Photo position

Evaluation

There are many positive aspects of Rolls Crescent:
- The varied building heights and the enhanced corner treatment help to create positive focal points along both sides of the street;
- Front doors face directly onto the street, improving public surveillance;
- There is a wide mix of dwelling types, tenure and size;

- The building line is behind a two-metre deep buffer zone, which provides space for rubbish, storage, meter boxes, cycles, and allows for personalisation. This design also reinforces the public/private divide.

Arguably a negative aspect of the development is the small size of private and communal gardens, although, the communal space does lend a sense of community to the development.

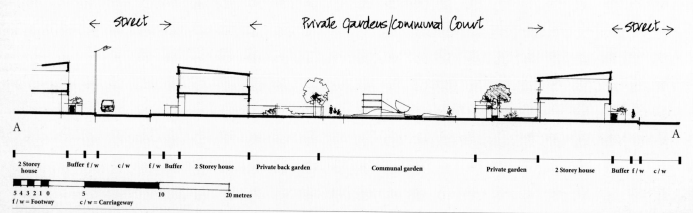

← street →   ← Private Gardens/Communal Court →   ← street →

A   A

2 Storey house   Buffer f/w   c/w   f/w   Buffer   2 Storey house   Private back garden   Communal garden   Private garden   2 Storey house   Buffer f/w   c/w

5 4 3 2 1 0   5   10   20 metres
f/w = Footway   c/w = Carriageway

❶ The site offers a varied mix of dwellings, including one-storey disabled units. On-street parking effectively reduces traffic speeds. There are only six off-street parking bays and these are designated for the disabled.

❷ Two metre wide zones in the front of buildings allow for bin storage, meter boxes, cycle storage and personalisation.

❸ Arising from the variety and mix of dwelling types, the roofscape presents an attractive skyline profile and creates interest from street level.

❹ There is a distinct buffer zone between the street and the building line.

❺ Internal courtyards provide small, overlooked, yet secure private gardens and a small comunal courtyard.

Analysis of built form components within the area of detailed analysis	
Area of detailed analysis:	1.23 ha.
Number of Dwellings (67 Houses):	67
Dwelling mix (11 dwelling types): 2-bed house	Houses: 2-bed houses (wheelchair accessible) 2-bed houses (3 types) 3-bed houses (5 types) 4-bed houses (wheelchair accessible) 5-bed houses
Density	
Dwellings per hectare:	54
Habitable rooms per hectare:	233
Floorspace per hectare:	4961.1m^2
Space in and around the home	
2-bed house:	80.5 m^2
Typical garden area for a 2-bed house:	
3-bed house:	95 m^2
Typical garden area for a 3-bed house:	48 m^2
Car Parking	
Parking spaces per dwelling:	0.8
Parking within building curtilage:	11%
On-street:	89%
Parking courts/ dedicated off-street bays:	0%
Garages	0%
Overall land budget	
Dwellings footprint:	28%
Private gardens:	33%
Communal outdoor space and courtyards:	9%
Roads, footpaths and parking:	30%

Greenland Passage, Southwark

Built
1988

Lead designer
Kjaer and Richter

Developer
Aarhus Ilsef UK

Local authority
London Borough of Southwark

Overview

Greenland Passage is located on the edge of Greenland Dock adjoining the River Thames, within London Docklands. Surrey Quays is the nearest local centre, which is approximately one kilometre from the development. The scheme combines the refinement of Danish construction with a typical British housing form. The development comprises two perimeter blocks, which include private and semi-private gardens.

A terrace of townhouses with integral garages and a nine-storey tower of flats also forms part of the area of detailed analysis. Car parking is located either within one of three underground car parks, or in the integral garages along Finland Street and South Sea Street.

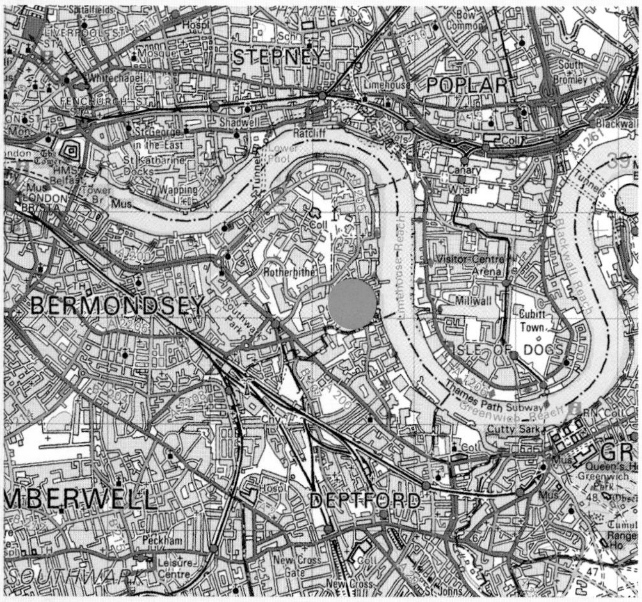

● The site

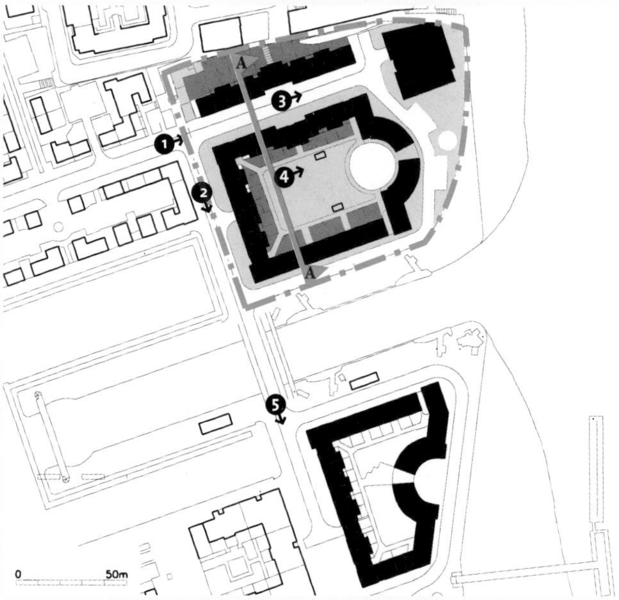

N

Area of detailed analysis

Photo position

Evaluation

A number of strong features can be identified:

- The scheme combines a permeable road network with two perimeter blocks which have partly enclosed courtyards;
- There is good pedestrian access into the site via Greenland Dock. Roads are unusually wide in places, up to eight metres;
- Housing types and designs are quite varied, yet Royal Court has a strong sense of enclosure and repose. This is partly due to the enclosure formed by the King Frederick Tower at the end of the vista and the use of three-storey townhouses;
- The scheme contains a very high proportion of designated parking spaces. One space per dwelling has been allocated as a combination of garages, both integral and underground;
- On-street parking provides additional spaces and allows for as many as two spaces per dwelling.

Nonetheless parking supply appears to be a significant issue in Greenland Passage. Some vehicles are parked on public open space along the Thames. The site is quite remote in its location from public transport, increasing dependency on the car.

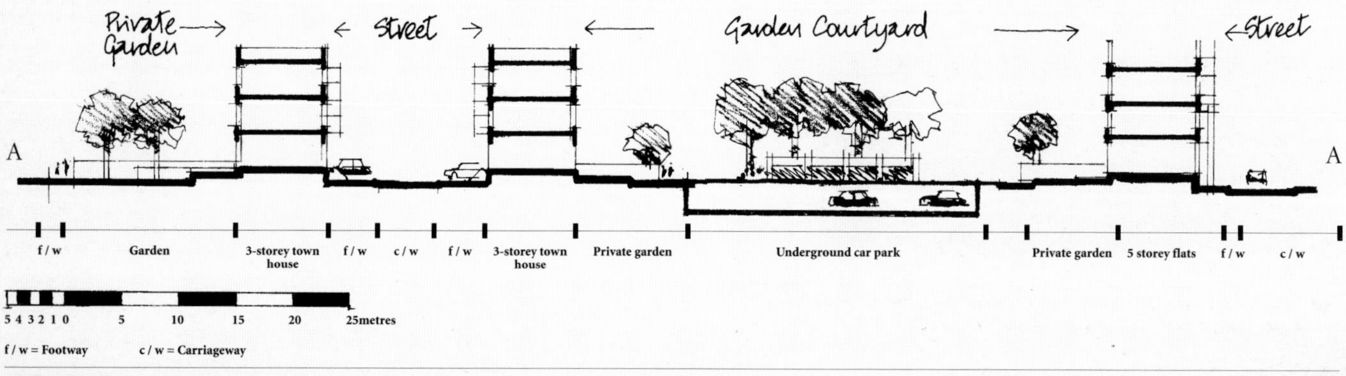

❶ There is good pedestrian access into the site via Greenland Dock. Roads are unusually wide in places and some are as much as eight metres.

❷ The development combines a permeable road network with two perimeter blocks which have partly enclosed courtyards.

❸ King Frederick Tower at the end of the vista and the three-storey town-houses along Royal Court help to create a sense of enclosure for the street.

❹ Lattice fencing fails to provide privacy to all private rear gardens. Only where mature planting has been added is there really a sense of privacy.

❺ A lack of clear distinction between public and private space has resulted in cars being parked on the footway.

Analysis of built form components within the area of detailed analysis	
Area of detailed analysis:	1.2 ha
Number of Dwellings:	82
Dwelling mix: (4 dwelling types)	1+2 - bed apartment 2+3 - bed duplex 3 - bed town hoses
Density	
Dwellings per hectare:	68 dwellings/ hectare
Habitable rooms per hectare:	233
Floorspace per hectare:	10,886m²
Space in and around the home	
3-bed townhouse in Royal Court:	159m²
Typical garden area:	69m²
3-bed townhouse in Queen of Denmark Court:	162m²
Typical garden area:	31m²
Car parking	
Parking spaces per dwelling:	2.1
Parking within building curtilage:	0%
On street:	53%
Parking courts/ dedicated off-street bays/shelters:	31%
Garages:	16%
Overall land budget	
Dwellings footprint:	23%
Private gardens:	11%
Communal outdoor space and courtyards:	35%
Roads, footpaths and parking:	31%

Isledon Village, London

Built 1992	New Islington & Hackney HA, Circle 33 Housing Trust, ASRA Greater London HA, Kingsland HA, KUSH HA, Am Viet HA, Arhag HA
Lead designer HTA Architects	
	Local authority London Borough of Islington
Developer Consortium	

Overview

Isledon Village is a 2.9 hectare site located in Finsbury Park in North London. The development contains 211 dwellings, which represents the relatively high density of 73 units per hectare, while offering a broad mix of tenures. Flats as well as large family homes provide residents with a range of lifestyle choices in the development. The scheme also includes a nursing home for elderly people, people with mental health

problems and disabled people, a self-built nursery, community facilities, a doctor's surgery, workspaces and open space incorporating a children's play area. The site was originally proposed as a National Fashion Centre, but through a community-led planning initiative, the Finsbury Park Action Group won planning permission for a mix of homes and jobs and a health and community centre.

● The site

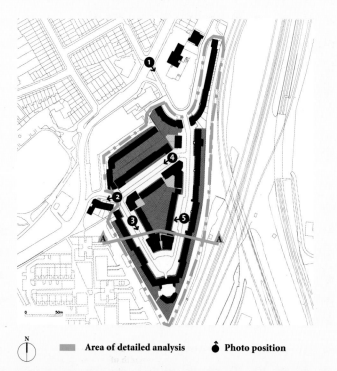

N ⊕ ▬ Area of detailed analysis   ● Photo position

Evaluation

Isledon Village has many positive features:
- A mix of tenure in blocks of flats, maisonettes and houses, with social housing to rent, shared ownership, home equity, and a nursing home for people with mental health problems;
- A high proportion of houses and flats have wheelchair access;
- Strong block structure and clear definition of public and private space. The block structure also prevents access into rear gardens, avoiding security issues;

- Different car parking techniques make a positive contribution to the street. Lateral tree planting encloses the street width, enhancing pedestrian priority.

The use of one-way streets is considered one of the main downsides of the development. A two-way movement would have slowed cars down further and enhanced the level of safety on the site.

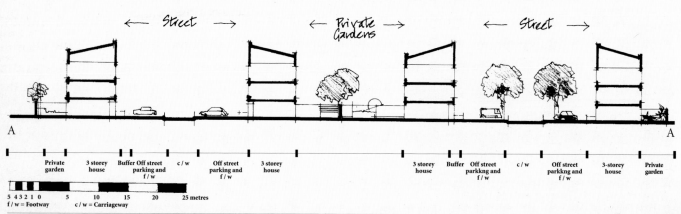

1 The scheme is a positive contribution to the surrounding streets and to a degree reduces the severance caused by Isledon Road.

2 One-way traffic flow increases vehicle speed, reducing the level of pedestrian safety, and adding to signage.

3 Varied parking provision, as well as lateral tree planting, extends the pedestrian zone and reduces the apparent width of the road. A combination of parking formats includes on-street and off-street parking.

4 There is a clear distinction between public and private space in the scheme.

5 Many of these two metre wide buffer zones display a high level of personalisation and maintenance, but due to the size of these gardens, those that are not attended to do have a detrimental effect on the environment as a whole.

Isledon Village, London

Analysis of built form components in the area of detailed analysis	
The site	
Area of detailed analysis:	2.9 ha
Number of dwellings: (60 Houses and 151 flats)	211
Dwelling mix: 10 dwelling types	Flats: 1,2,3+4 bed flats with wheelchair access 1,2,3,4 and 6 bed houses
Density	
Dwellings per hectare:	73
Habitable rooms per hectare:	238
Floorspace per hectare:	8036 m²
Space in and around the home	
2 bed apartment:	69.5m²
Typical garden area for a ground floor flat:	38 m²
Typical garden area for an upper level flat:	None/share of communal garden
3-bed house:	104m²
Typical garden area for a 3-bed house:	50-88 m²
Car parking	
Parking spaces per dwelling:	1.1
Parking within building curtilage:	6.5%
On-street:	37%
Parking courts/ dedicated off street bays:	50%
Garages:	6.5%
Overall land budget	
Dwellings footprint:	32%
Private gardens:	25%
Communal outdoor space and courtyards:	22%
Roads, footpaths and parking:	22%

Deansgate Quay, Manchester

Built
2000

Lead Designer
Stephenson Bell Ltd

Developer
Crosby Homes (North West)Ltd

Local authority
Manchester City Council

Overview

Deansgate Quay is located in the heart of Manchester City Centre at the edge of the Castlefield regeneration area. The site lies between the A57(M) and the railway; the one hectare site is almost bisected by the Bridgewater Canal.

The seven-storey building, contains 102 one, two and three bedroom apartments and maisonettes.

● The site

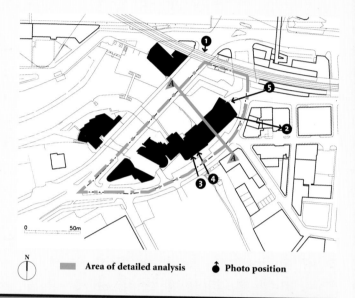

N ▮ **Area of detailed analysis** ⚲ **Photo position**

0   50m

Evaluation

Densgate Quay has many positive attributes:
- The development sits well in its robust context. Its form, scale and massing fit comfortably with the large and confident historic industrial buildings;
- Large windows offer attractive views out of the site, but can lead to issues of detailed design. On occasions personalisation has lead to aesthetic problems;
- Although the site does not contain any open space, the scheme attempts to give each dwelling its own balcony. A floating island for wildlife is proposed on the Canal;

- Private car parking spaces are not allocated to each dwelling, but are purchased separately. The majority of car parking spaces are located in dedicated bays; and some car spaces have been tucked out of sight under the railway arches. Offices located on the ground floor create natural surveillance and promote activity around the site during the day.

A significant shortcoming however is the addition of a poorly designed parking deck which seriously undermines the quality of the scheme.

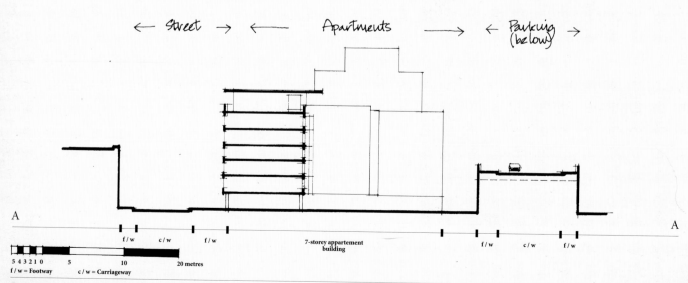

← Street → ← Apartments → ← Parking (below) →

A   A

f/w   c/w   f/w   7-storey appartement building   f/w   c/w   f/w

5 4 3 2 1 0   5   10   20 metres
f/w = Footway   c/w = Carriageway

❶ Deansgate Quay sits comfortably in the context of its histroic industrial urban fabric

❷ Large windows offer attractive outlooks to the Castlefield Quarter.

❸ Large windows can lead to visual problems when flats are personalised.

❹ Private car parking spaces are not allocated to each dwelling, but are purchased separately.

❺ A poorly designed parking deck undermines the scheme and removes privacy from first floor apartments.

Analysis of built form components within the area of detailed analysis	
Area of detailed analysis:	1 ha
Number of Dwellings:	102
Dwelling mix (5 dwelling types):	1-bed, 2 & 3-bed apartments 2 & 3-bed duplex apartments
Density	
Dwellings per hectare:	102
Habitable rooms per hectare:	278
Floorspace per hectare:	9954 m^2
Space in and around the home	
2-bed apartment:	71 m^2
Typical garden area for a 2-bed:	3 m^2
3-bed apartment:	164 m^2
Typical garden area 3-bed:	36 m^2
Car Parking	
Parking spaces per dwelling:	0.8
Parking within building curtilage:	0%
On-street:	0%
Parking courts/ dedicated off-street bays/shelters:	91%
Garages:	8%
Overall land budget	
Dwellings footprint:	15%
Private gardens: (NB does not include balconies)	0%
Communal outdoor space and courtyards:	0%
Roads, footpaths and parking:	85%

Deansgate Quay, Manchester

Webster's Yard, Kendal

Built
1987

Lead designer
Mike Walford Architects

Developer
Russell Armer

Local authority
South Lakeland District Council

Overview

Webster's Yard is located in the centre of Kendal. The three-storey development follows the pattern of existing lanes and yards, which run in an east-west direction from Highgate. Sixty-two dwellings are provided by the development and 40 of them are for sheltered housing. The scheme comprises a series of long, narrow courtyards with a pedestrian passage running through the centre. The main entry into the site is through a pedestrian gate opening from Highgate. An underground car park provides parking spaces for 29 cars, allocated to the 24 private dwellings. Traditional materials are used to create a scheme which is successfully in keeping with its context.

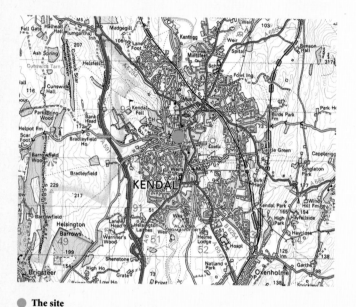

● The site

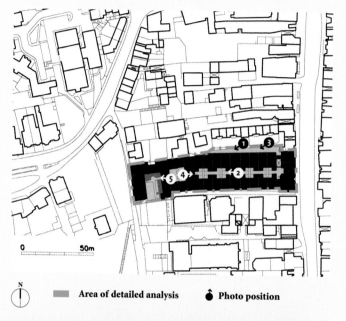

Ⓝ   ▬ Area of detailed analysis   ● Photo position

0   50m

Evaluation

Positive aspects of the scheme include:

- A good range of different housing types including a combination of houses, flats and sheltered housing units;
- Its east-west orientation maximises views to the south and north. Landscaping in the adjacent Almshouses Sandes' Hospital Cottages, and the position of Webster's Yard relevant to the adjacent yards helps to improve views from the windows and balconies within the development;
- The provision of attractive outdoor spaces in the form of semi-private communal gardens and courtyards.

It is unfortunate however that some of the architect's original details have been compromised during the construction process.

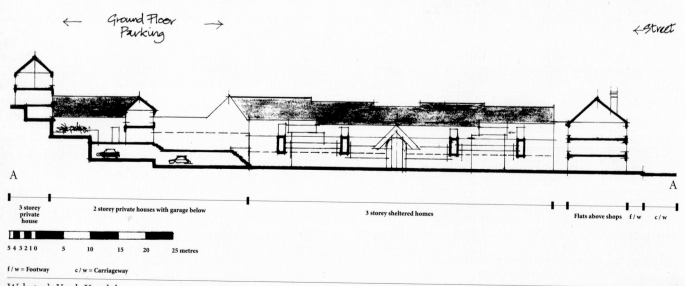

← Ground Floor Parking →

←Street

A

A

3 storey private house

2 storey private houses with garage below

3 storey sheltered homes

Flats above shops   f/w   c/w

5 4 3 2 1 0   5   10   15   20   25 metres

f/w = Footway   c/w = Carriageway

❶ The scheme provides a good range of housing types, including a combination of houses, flats and sheltered housing units.

❷ Raised walkways and 'deck access' work well in this case, given the intimate nature of the scheme.

❸ Adjoining yards enhance views from the site.

❹ Semi-private and communal gardens and courtyards are features of this high density, town centre site.

❺ Some of the architect's original details have been compromised during the design-and-build process, but the Dowker Arch in the lower courtyard is closer to the original design.

Analysis of built form components within the area of detailed analysis	
Area detailed analysis:	0.35 hectares
Number of Dwellings: (40 Sheltered homes, 8 houses, 6 flats and 8 flats above shops)	62
Dwelling mix: 4 dwellings types	Sheltered homes Houses and flats in upper/lower yards Flats above shops
Density	
Dwellings per hectare:	177
Habitable rooms per hectare:	477
Floorspace per hectare:	11,658 m²
Space in and around the home	
3-bed house:	117m²
Typical garden area:	22 m²
2-bed apartment:	62 m²
Typical garden area for a ground floor flat + upper flat:	Access to communal courtyard & garden
Car parking	
Parking spaces per dwelling:	1.2 (for private housing only)
Parking within building curtiliage:	0%
On-street:	0%
Parking courts/ dedicated off-street bays:	0%
Basement garage:	100%
Overall land budget	
Dwellings footprint:	60%
Private gardens:	4%
Communal outdoor space and courtyards:	23%
Roads, footpaths and parking:	13%

Further Reading [1]

Aldous, T. (1992) *Urban Villages*, London, Urban Villages Group.

Association of Chief Police Officers (1999) *Secured by Design Standards*, London, ACPO.

Bentley, I. et al (1985) *Responsive Environments: a manual for designers*, London, Architectural Press.

Birmingham City Council (2001) *Places for Living: Revised Residential Design Guide for Birmingham*, Birmingham, Department of Planning and Architecture.

Brewerton, J. & David, D. (1997) *Designing Lifetime Homes*, York, Joseph Rowntree Foundation.

Building Research Establishment (1995) *Environmental Standard: Homes for a Greener World*, London, BRE.

Burnett, J. (1978) *A Social History of Housing 1815-1970*, London, Routeledge.

Calthorpe, P. (1993) *The Next American Metropolis: Ecology, Community and the American Dream*, New York, Princeton Architectural Press.

Carmona, M. (2001) *Housing Design Quality: through policy, guidance and review*, London, Spon.

Chambers, J. (1985) *The English House*, London, Methuen London Ltd.

Colquhoun, I. (1999) *RIBA Book of 20th Century British Housing*, Oxford, Butterworth-Heinemann.

Colquhoun, I. & Fauset, P. (1991) *Housing Design in Practice*, Harlow, Longmans.

Colquhoun, I. & Fauset, P. (1991) *Housing Design: An International Perspective*, London, B.T. Batsford Ltd.

County Surveyors Society, (1999) *Code of Good Practice for Street lighting*, London, Institution of Lighting Engineers.

Daunton, M.J. (1983) *House and Home in the Victorian City*, London, Edward Arnold.

DETR (1998) *Planning for Sustainable Development: Towards Better Practice*, London, DETR.

DETR (1998) *The Use of Density in Urban Planning*, London, DETR.

DETR (1998) *A New Deal for Transport Better for Everyone, The Government's White Paper on the Future of Transport*, London, The Stationery Office.

DETR (1998) *Places, Streets and Movement, A Companion Guide to Design Bulletin 32*, (Residential Roads and Footpaths), London, DETR.

DETR (2000) *Planning Policy Guidance Note 3: Housing*, London, DETR.

DETR (2000) *Our Towns and Cities: the future - Delivering an urban renaissance*, London, The Stationery Office.

DETR (2000) *Our Countryside: the future - A fair deal for rural England*, London, The Stationery Office.

DETR (2001) *Planning Policy Guidance Note 13: Transport*, London, DETR.

DETR & CABE (2000) *By Design: urban design in the planning system - towards better practice*, London, Thomas Telford Publishing.

DETR & DTI (1999) *Planning for Passive Solar Design*, Watford, BRECSU & BRE.

DETR & Housing Corporation (1999) *Housing Quality Indicators: Research Report and Indicators*, London, DETR.

DETR, RIBA, RTPI & NHBC (1997 -2001) *Home A Place to Live: Housing Design Awards*, Birmingham, Housing Design Awards Office.

English Partnerships and the Housing Corporation (2000) *Urban Design Compendium*, London, English Partnerships.

Frey, H. (1999) *Designing the City Towards a More Sustainable Urban Form*, London, E & FN Spon.

Guinness Trust (1996) *Planning and Architecture Guide*, High Wycombe, Guinness Trust.

Guinness Trust (undated) *Landscape and Design Guide*, High Wycombe, Guinness Trust.

Hall, P. and Ward, C. (1998) *Sociable Cities*, Chichester, John Wiley.

National Housing Federation (1998) *Car Parking and Social Housing*, London, National Housing Federation.

Harris, R. & Larkham, P. (1999) *Changing Suburbs: Foundation, Form and Function*, London, E & FN Spon.

Hass-Klau, C. et al (1992) *Civilised Streets: a Guide to Traffic Calming*, Brighton, Environmental and Transport Planning.

Hulme Regeneration Limited (1994), *Rebuilding the City: A Guide to Development in Hulme*, Manchester, Hulme Regeneration Ltd.

Jackson, A. (1973). *Semi-Detached London*, Didcot, Wild Swan.

Joseph Rowntree Foundation (1995) *Made to Last: Creating Sustainable Neighbourhoods and Estate Regeneration*, Joseph Rowntree Foundation.

Karn, V. & Sheridan L. (1998) *Housing Quality: A Practical Guide for Tenants and Their Representatives*, York, Joseph Rowntree Foundation.

Katz P. (1994) *The New Urbanism: Towards an Architecture of the Community*, New York, McGraw-Hill.

London Planning Advisory Committee (1998) *Sustainable Residential Quality: New Approaches to Urban Living*, London, LPAC.

London Planning Advisory Committee (2000) *Sustainable Residential Quality: Exploring the Housing Potential of Large Sites*, London, LPAC.

Lynch, K. (1984) *Good City Form*, Massachusetts, MIT Press.

Lynch, K. (1990) *The Image of the City*, Massachusetts, MIT Press.

Manchester City Council (1997) *A Guide to Development in Manchester*, Manchester, Department of Planning.

Muthesius, S. (1982) *The English Terraced House*, New Haven / London, Yale University Press.

National Housing Federation (1998) *Standards and Quality in Development: A Good Practice Guide*, London, National Housing Federation.

National Housing Federation and Home Trust (1993) *Accommodating Diversity: Housing Design in Multicultural Society*, London, National Housing Federation.

Oliver, P., Davis, I., & Bentley, I. (1981) *Dunroamin: The Suburban Semi and its Enemies*, London, Barrie & Jenkins Ltd.

Osborn, S. & Shaftoe, H. (1995) *Safer Neighbourhoods? Successes and Failures in Crime Prevention*, Safe Neighbourhoods Unit.

Pascoe, T. (1999) *Evaluation of Secured By Design in Public Sector Housing*, London, BRE & DETR.

Pharoah T. (1993) *Traffic Calming Guidelines*, Exeter, Devon County Council.

Prince's Foundation, English Partnerships, DETR & CPRE (2000) *Sustainable Urban Extensions: planned through design*, London, The Prince's Foundation.

Rogers, R. (1997) *Cities for a Small Planet*, London, Faber and Faber.

Rogers, R. (2000) *Cities for a Small Country*, London, Faber and Faber.

Rudlin, D. & Falk, N. (1999) *Building the 21st Century Home: The Sustainable Urban Neighbourhood*, Oxford, Butterworth-Heinemann.

Saint, A. et al, (1999) *London Suburbs*, London, Merrell Holberton Publishers Ltd.

Scottish Enterprise (1997) *Streets Ahead*, Glasgow, Scottish Enterprise.

Scottish Environmental Protection Agency (2000) *Watercourses in the Community: a guide to sustainable watercourse management in the urban environment*, Stirling, SEPA.

Sherlock, H. (1991) *Cities Are Good For Us*, Glasgow, Paladin.

TRL consultants (2001), *A Road Safety Good Practice Guide*, London, DETR.

Urban Design Group (2000) *The Community Planning Handbook*, London, Earthscan.

Urban Task Force (1999) *Towards an Urban Renaissance*, London, E&FN Spon.

Wines, J. (2000) *Green Architecture*, London, Taschen.

1 This list of further reading is not intended to represent a comprehensive listing of all the publications relevant to housing layout and design. Other relevant publications are listed in the further reading sections of By Design, the Urban Design Compendium and in many of the other publications set out above. The inclusion of publications here does not imply any endorsement on the part of either DTLR or CABE to their content.

Acknowledgements

Better Places to Live: By Design was prepared by consultants Llewelyn-Davies in association with Alan Baxter & Associates.

The consultants would like to thank the many people and organisations who have contributed to the guide, both as specialist advisors and as members of the Sounding Board which was convened to advise the project. Thanks are also due to officials at both the DTLR and CABE who acted as the Steering Group for the project.

Image Credits

Beechcroft, page 72 (bottom)
Countryside Properties, page 83 (image 4)
Duchy of Cornwall, page 18
The Geo Information Group, page 10
HTA, page 25 (image 2)
HTA, page 39
HTA, page 41 (bottom right)
Jestico + Whiles, page 74 (bottom left)
Local Authorities of South Yorkshire (diagrams page 25)
Peabody Trust , page 69
Peter Cook/ VIEW, page 4
Peter Cook/VIEW, page73 (bottom left)
Peter Cook/VIEW, page77 (top right)
Phil Sayer, page 8 (right)
Phil Sayer, page 61
Phil Sayer, page 63 (right)
Phil Sayer, page 64 (left)
PRP Architects, page 35 (bottom left)
Shillam & Smith, page 68
TC Communications, page 11 (bottom right)
TC Communications, page 63 (images 1 & 2 right)

All other images Llewelyn-Davies/Alan Baxter & Associates

Ordnance Survey Mapping

All mapping is reproduced from the OS map by the Department for Transport, Local Government and the Regions with the permission of the Ordnance Survey on behalf of The Controller of Her Majesty's Stationery Office (c) Crown copyright. All rights reserved. Unauthorised reproduction infringes Crown Copyright and may lead to prosecution or civil proceedings. Licence Number GD272671.